THE LIBRARY OF
AMERICAN
LIVES AND TIMES™

HARRIET BEECHER STOWE

Author and Abolitionist

Ryan P. Randolph

The Rosen Publishing Group's
PowerPlus Books™
New York

For my mother, Lynda Randolph, with love.

Published in 2004 by The Rosen Publishing Group, Inc.
29 East 21st Street, New York, NY 10010

First Edition

Editor's Note: All quotations have been reproduced as they appeared in the letters and diaries from which they were borrowed. No correction was made to the inconsistent spelling that was common in that time period.

Library of Congress Cataloging-in-Publication Data

Randolph, Ryan P.
Harriet Beecher Stowe : author and abolitionist / Ryan P. Randolph.
   p. cm. — (The library of American lives and times)
Summary: A biography of the nineteenth-century author whose anti-slavery novel "Uncle Tom's Cabin" helped intensify the disagreement between North and South.
Includes bibliographical references and index.
   ISBN 0-8239-6623-2 (lib. bdg.)
1. Stowe, Harriet Beecher, 1811–1896—Juvenile literature. 2. Stowe, Harriet Beecher, 1811–1896. Uncle Tom's cabin—Juvenile literature. 3. United States—History—Civil War, 1861–1865—Literature and the war—Juvenile literature. 4. Authors, American—19th century—Biography—Juvenile literature. 5. Abolitionists—United States—Biography—Juvenile literature. 6. Suffragists—United States—Biography—Juvenile literature. 7. Slavery in literature—Juvenile literature. [1. Stowe, Harriet Beecher, 1811–1896. 2. Authors, American. 3. Abolitionists. 4. Women—Biography.] I. Title. II. Series.
   PS2956 .R36 2004
   813'.3—dc21

                                                    2002007041

Manufactured in the United States of America

CONTENTS

1. Author and Abolitionist

The United States of America was experiencing a great deal of change during the nineteenth century. America had established itself as a new and independent republic in the late 1700s, but the nation was still struggling with its national identity. Americans were learning how to balance the needs and rights of individuals with the needs of a growing country.

It was into this environment that Harriet Beecher Stowe was born, and it enabled her to make a lasting impact on the thoughts and ideas that were shaping America. The issues of slavery and women's rights were quickly moving to the forefront of American awareness. Through her novels, Harriet Beecher Stowe would help many Americans understand these issues by placing them in the realm of everyday life.

Harriet Beecher Stowe was one of the most successful writers of her time. She was especially famous for writing

Opposite page: At the start of her career, Harriet Beecher Stowe wrote to her husband, "If I am to write, I must have a room to myself, which shall be *my* room." The National Bank Note Company created this Civil War–era engraving of Stowe.

Uncle Tom's Cabin; or, Life Among the Lowly, a novel published in 1852 that showed the evils of slavery. The novel sold three hundred thousand copies in the first year and was eventually translated into more than sixty languages. The only book that sold more copies that year was the Bible.

The fact that her book sold so many copies is an excellent indicator that the topic of slavery was on everyone's mind. Most people in the North were against the practice, but many people in the South felt that their way of life would be destroyed without it. Economics rather than morality largely influenced both viewpoints, however.

Northerners believed that if slavery were allowed to spread to the new territories that were opening up for settlement in the West, there would be fewer opportunities for the industries and individuals in the North to make money. Although the southern economy had remained largely agricultural, the northern economy had branched into industries such as textiles. Why would someone pay a person a wage for his or her work if a system was in place that allowed slavery? Southerners felt that if slavery was forbidden in these new territories, southern farmers would have to pay more for labor. This would completely alter their economy.

The idea that slavery should be abolished for moral reasons, rather than just economic ones, was less widely held. Even northerners tended to feel that whites were superior to blacks, but they also believed in the idea of a

$200 Reward.

RANAWAY from the subscriber, on the night of Thursday, the 30th of Sepember,

FIVE NEGRO SLAVES,

To-wit : one Negro man, his wife, and three children.

The man is a black negro, full height, very erect, his face a little thin.   He is about forty years of age, and calls himself *Washington Reed*, and is known by the name of Washington.   He is probably well dressed, possibly takes with him an ivory headed cane, and is of good address.   Several of his teeth are gone.

Mary, his wife, is about thirty years of age, a bright mulatto woman, and quite stout and strong.

The oldest of the children is a boy, of the name of FIELDING, twelve years of age, a dark mulatto, with heavy eyelids.   He probably wore a new cloth cap.

MATILDA, the second child, is a girl, six years of age, rather a dark mulatto, but a bright and smart looking child.

MALCOLM, the youngest, is a boy, four years old, a lighter mulatto than the last, and about equally as bright.   He probably also wore a cloth cap.   If examined, he will be found to have a swelling at the navel.

Washington and Mary have lived at or near St. Louis, with the subscriber, for about 15 years.

It is supposed that they are making their way to Chicago, and that a white man accompanies them, that they will travel chiefly at night, and most probably in a covered wagon.

A reward of $150 will be paid for their apprehension, so that I can get them, if taken within one hundred miles of St. Louis, and $200 if taken beyond that, and secured so that I can get them, and other reasonable additional charges, if delivered to the subscriber, or to THOMAS ALLEN, Esq., at St. Louis, Mo. The above negroes, for the last few years, have been in possession of Thomas Allen, Esq., of St. Louis.

WM. RUSSELL.

ST. LOUIS, Oct. 1, 1847.

This 1847 poster advertises a reward for the return of an escaped slave family. The 1850 Fugitive Slave Act allowed slave owners, bounty hunters, and law enforcement officers to pursue escaped slaves into a free state to capture them.

free market economy, in which everyone who worked should be paid for their efforts. Abolitionist groups were growing, however. These groups worked hard to eliminate slavery, arguing that it was an evil, cruel practice.

Harriet Beecher Stowe had witnessed the cruelties of slavery firsthand. She was also active in the same social circles as many abolitionists. Her thoughts were influenced by these interactions and experiences. At the urging of her family, she decided to write something about the horrors of slavery. The daughter of a preacher, she was no stranger to presenting a story that brought home a moral lesson. She had already written essays on religion and many magazine articles on the home and daily life in America. These articles taught her to communicate information to average Americans, not just to the wealthy or educated. Harriet Beecher Stowe was extremely well suited to help Americans see and understand the immorality of the slave system.

Harriet Beecher Stowe was also remarkable in that she worked for a living and helped to support her family in a time when such tasks were generally left to men. She had received a formal education, and with her sister she helped to bring similar opportunities to other American women. The education of most women at this time in America was rather informal. They were taught at home, learning the basic skills needed to run a household. Men, however, were sent to formal schools. Harriet Beecher Stowe found herself promoting women's rights, as well as championing those of enslaved blacks.

Her achievements have earned Harriet Beecher Stowe an honored place in America's history. Her exclamation, "I will write something. I will if I live," has echoed through the years to reach the countless people who have read her works. She did live and she did write, about slavery and about many other topics relevant to her time.

2. A Religious Childhood

On June 14, 1811, the Beecher family welcomed Harriet Elizabeth Beecher into their home in Litchfield, Connecticut. It was a busy household that was full of life. Harriet Beecher was the sixth of eleven children in her family. Lyman and Roxana Foote Beecher, Harriet's parents, also opened their house to relatives, had two servants, and rented rooms in their house to boarders. Lyman and Roxana would have seven children together. Later, Lyman and his second wife, Harriet Porter, would increase the family by having four more children.

Lyman Beecher raised his children to form their own opinions. He was noted for being "the father of more brains than any other man in America."

Roxana Foote Beecher, Harriet's mother, was a well educated, intelligent woman and the granddaughter of

Roxana Foote Beecher was an avid reader. Ever busy with her housework and family, she would read while at the spinning wheel.

the Revolutionary War general Andrew Ward. Unfortunately, childbirth and the demands of running such a hectic household weakened Roxana Beecher. She became ill, and in 1816, she died of tuberculosis. Although Harriet was just five years old at the time, the influence and memory of her mother would appear in some of her later works.

Many of Harriet's memories of her mother were shaped by how Lyman Beecher and her older brothers and sisters remembered Roxana. Harriet later wrote that her father often "spoke of mother" when he "wished to make an appeal to our hearts." This led Harriet to suggest that her mother's memory "had more influence in moulding her family, in deterring from evil and exciting to good, than the living presence of many mothers." Perhaps just as important, Harriet's intelligence, love of reading, and open mind were all traits from her mother and the Foote family.

Lyman Beecher was the energetic head of the Beecher family. Beecher was born in 1775, and his father and grandfather were both blacksmiths. He went to Yale College in New Haven, Connecticut. In 1799, Lyman Beecher was ordained a minister, just as America was

BPMS MEDIA CENTER

The town of Litchfield, Connecticut, served as a depot that held ammunition and supplies during the American Revolution. Litchfield was located between Boston and New York City. In the days before high-speed trains, airplanes, and cars, many people stayed in Litchfield on their travels between the two cities. The town had theaters, schools, libraries, and other institutions. The prosperity of the town, as well as the growth of liberal ideals that encouraged women's rights, provided new opportunities for the education of women that were not available in many other regions of the United States.

entering a period known as the Second Great Awakening. This was a time of religious revival. Americans were awakening to religion and attending church more frequently. Lyman Beecher was determined to play a significant role in American religious life. As a preacher he would spread the teachings of Jesus contained in the New Testament.

One year before Harriet Beecher's birth, Lyman Beecher moved from his first church in East Hampton, Long Island, to Litchfield, Connecticut, to serve as the pastor of a local church. He was known for his stamina, confidence, and intelligence. His years as a pastor in Litchfield would bring Lyman Beecher some degree of national fame.

This decorative wood panel adorned Lyman Beecher's pulpit when he was the pastor at the First Congregational Church in Litchfield, Connecticut. A pulpit is a raised platform, where a preacher stands to give his sermons.

The religion that Lyman Beecher preached was a strict, or fundamental, form of Calvinism, a Christian religion. Calvinism is a set of Christian religious beliefs that is known for being particularly strict in its requirements for following the faith. Calvinist ministers also urged congregations to work hard and to avoid wasteful spending. Lyman Beecher gave booming sermons on the necessity of strong faith, and he became renowned for his sermons and writings against drinking alcohol.

The messages in Lyman Beecher's fiery sermons reached right into the Beecher household. The entire family was influenced by his teachings. He challenged his children to debate religious ideas, ask questions, and think seriously about religion. He thought this would help his children to embrace his religious views. In reality, many of Lyman Beecher's children rejected his strict brand of Calvinism for more moderate forms. They did, however, learn to debate ideas and to question why things were the way they were. This left the Beecher children with strong wills and opened the way to promising futures.

Harriet spent almost a year living with her aunt and grandmother in the Nutplains area of Guilford, Connecticut. The Guilford Green is one of the largest town greens in New England. In the nineteenth century, the women of Guilford would gather each spring to remove the leaves that had fallen over the winter. The Green, shown here, is still in use today.

Growing up, Harriet Beecher often escaped the strict religious atmosphere of Lyman Beecher's house by visiting her aunt, Harriet Foote, and her grandmother Roxana Foote in the Nutplains area of Guilford, Connecticut. Nutplains was the childhood home of Harriet's mother, Roxana.

The Foote family was wealthier than the Beecher family, and from the Footes Harriet learned proper manners as well as the domestic arts of sewing and knitting. Harriet later recalled of her Aunt Harriet, "A more energetic human being never undertook the education of a child." At Nutplains, Harriet had more access to books, novels, and poetry. At home her father occasionally restricted what his children were allowed to read. Harriet's visits were remembered as the "golden hours" of her childhood.

Harriet Beecher's memories of her times in Nutplains were always vivid. She wrote, "Every juniperbush, every wild sweetbrier, every barren sandy hillside, every stony pasture, spoke of bright hours of love, when we were welcomed back to Nutplains as to our mother's heart."

It is not known just how many trips or how much time Harriet Beecher spent in Nutplains, but it is thought that she spent a good deal of time there between Roxana's death in 1816 and Lyman Beecher's marriage in 1817 to his second wife, Harriet Porter. Harriet Porter was very much like Roxana in that she was educated and intelligent. The Beecher children, including Harriet Beecher, liked their stepmother, but she was not closely involved in their care and she did not displace the strong memory of their mother.

Harriet Porter gave birth to four additional Beecher children. She realized how intelligent the Beecher children were and wrote in a letter, "Harriet and Henry . . . are always hand-in-hand. They are as lovely children as I ever saw, amiable, affectionate, and very bright."

Both in Nutplains and at the Beecher household, Harriet and her family were avid readers. For a time, Lyman Beecher declared novels "trash," but he and the family soon became fans of Sir Walter Scott, author of novels such as *Ivanhoe*. As did many Americans, the Beechers also read the works of Lord Byron and closely followed the scandals in his real life. The romantic, or dramatic and sentimental, style of these writers would later influence the style in which Harriet would write. Harriet Beecher and her brothers and sisters began their education at home with the books they read and with the ideas that they debated and discussed as a family.

3. School Life

In addition to the knowledge that she gained at home, in 1819, Harriet Beecher began her formal education. Lyman Beecher enrolled Harriet at Miss Pierce's School, in Litchfield, in exchange for his services as a pastor. The school usually accepted only young women who were at least twelve years old, but Harriet was accepted at eight years old because of her mental maturity and intelligence.

Miss Pierce's School was established for the education of young women. Schools for women did exist across the United States, but they were not widely available. In fact, for the most part, only wealthy families could afford to educate their daughters formally. In the late 1700s, many women were not educated. Some women studied the basics of reading and writing at home. Home education focused on domestic, or household, tasks, such as cooking, sewing, washing, and sometimes the management of the family's money. New England had a better record than most regions of the United States for educating young women because the Puritans, who began

Miss Sarah Pierce first began holding classes for young women in her dining room in 1792. Six years later, citizens of Litchfield, Connecticut, funded the building of the Litchfield Female Academy. Napoleon Gimbrede is believed to have created this watercolor, *View of the Litchfield Female Academy*, around 1830.

settling there in the seventeenth century, believed that all children should be able to read the Bible.

By the time Harriet Beecher began her schooling, more young women were learning to read and write. Female academies such as Miss Pierce's School were part of the reason for this increase in the literacy of women. At the time of Harriet's attendance, Miss Pierce's School was well known across the United States and had taught students from different areas of the country.

Sarah Pierce established the school to teach young women "the art of thinking." The school provided a classical education in which young women studied English literature, grammar, history, geography, mathematics, and sometimes Latin. Sarah Pierce's goal was to demonstrate "the equality of the female intellect."

Harriet Beecher stood out at such a young age because she was intelligent and learned quickly. In 1819, Lyman Beecher wrote a letter to a family member that read, "Harriet is a great genius—I would give a hundred dollars if she was a boy & Henry a girl—She is odd—as she is intelligent and studious." Despite the fact that Harriet was not a boy, as her father wished, her talent as a writer would one day bring her international fame.

In 1824, Harriet Beecher continued her studies at the Hartford Female Seminary in Hartford, Connecticut. Catharine Beecher, Harriet Beecher's older sister, had started this female academy in 1823 with just seven students. Catharine realized that for women there were few schools like Miss Pierce's School, and she sought to ensure that women

As a schoolgirl, Catharine Beecher was not a serious student. Of her early education she wrote that whatever she had managed to learn must have "walked into her head." This photo was taken around 1860.

When Harriet attended the Hartford Female Seminary in 1824, there was no school dormitory. Students boarded with local families. Harriet stayed with the Bull family, and for the first time in her life she had a room to herself. This is an etching of the school from around 1862.

such as her younger sisters would receive the education that they would need as adults.

The Hartford Female Seminary was modeled on Miss Pierce's School, but it also expanded on some of its ideas. Catharine strongly believed that women should receive a higher education. To do this, Catharine worked to make the curriculum, or subjects taught, similar to the subjects taught at men's colleges. In addition to reading, writing, history, geography, Latin, and arithmetic, young women were taught natural philosophy, including chemistry, physics, and astronomy. Her educational concepts and teaching methods spread to different women's schools across the nation.

Catharine developed another new teaching technique. She allowed older students to teach many subjects to the younger students. These older assistant teachers learned subjects better by teaching them, and they also gained a feeling of accomplishment and independence. Harriet Beecher was quickly made an assistant teacher for various subjects, including Latin, which she and Catharine learned from textbooks.

After Harriet Beecher finished her studies at the Hartford Female Seminary, she went to live with her family in Boston. The Beechers had moved to Massachusetts in 1826, when Lyman Beecher accepted a job as a pastor there. Harriet had now received a full education, but she had yet to find an outlet for her skills.

In fact, the options for many of the women graduating from female institutions were few, beyond teaching or becoming mothers and housewives. Women were not allowed to attend the all-male colleges where men learned to be doctors or lawyers, and very few women were involved in the business world. Catharine Beecher felt that an educated woman could run her household more efficiently and could raise better children. She also felt that if a woman chose not to marry, she should be prepared to live an independent life. In any case, the growing number of highly educated, intelligent women

MAP DRAWING.   13

LESSON II.

MAP DRAWING.

If you should travel *north* a great many days, you would come to a place that looks like this picture. These cliffs, that run up so high, are mountains of ice and snow which

After the American Revolution, geography gained prominence as a school subject. Students were taught to identify the vast holdings of their new nation, as well as the other regions of the world. This page from the Beechers' *Primary Geography for Children*, illustrated by E. Latella, depicts a scene from the North Pole.

Catharine Beecher found that the text-books available for the teaching of geography were rather poor. When she and Harriet later moved to Cincinnati, Ohio, they developed their own geography textbook. They decided to accompany the facts that needed to be taught with illustrative stories, quotations, and bits of conversation that would make the subject more interesting to children. Harriet wrote most of the book that she and Catharine conceived together. In 1833, Primary Geography for Children *was published, and many copies were sold to schools around the United States.*

would initiate the beginning of the women's rights movement in the mid-1800s.

With few friends in Boston and with little interest yet, at fifteen years old, in getting married or becoming a mother, Harriet Beecher became depressed. She wrote to Catharine that she often felt "So useless, so weak, so destitute of all energy." Catharine suggested to Lyman Beecher that Harriet return to Hartford. In November 1827, Harriet Beecher returned to the Hartford Female Seminary, this time as a teacher. Harriet would contribute to the family income through teaching until her marriage in 1836.

Back in Hartford, her job as a teacher kept her busy. Harriet Beecher mainly taught composition, or writing, but she also taught Latin and other subjects. She wrote, "I am quite buisy [sic] preparing for my Composition class. Have been reading Rasselas—& writing a little in imitation of Dr. Johnson's style—Think it is improving me by giving a command of the language."

When she was not teaching others, Harriet Beecher taught herself French and Italian and how to paint and draw. She also made new friends, including Mary Dutton, a math teacher at the school, and Georgiana May, who was also a teacher at the school. Harriet rode horses, took long walks, and talked with her friends. She exchanged letters with Georgiana for many years and even named one of her daughters Georgiana May.

Harriet's daughter, Georgiana May Stowe, was named in honor of Harriet's brother George and her friend Georgiana May Sykes. Harriet's daughter, shown in a photo from around 1865, was nicknamed Georgie.

In 1829, Catharine grew tired from her work at the Hartford Female Seminary, and she put the teachers in charge. This experience offered Harriet and the other teachers a chance to work together and act as leaders, and it gave Harriet confidence in her abilities. Harriet gave speeches to the students and teachers of the school on religion and morals. She also began to write letters to friends and family on the same subjects. Teaching composition classes and writing her sermons gave Harriet practice in the style of writing that she would later use in *Uncle Tom's Cabin*.

4. West to Cincinnati

Harriet Beecher's education at Miss Pierce's School and the Hartford Female Seminary was just part of the equation that would inspire Harriet to write her most famous book. In 1832, Harriet would move west with her family to Cincinnati, Ohio. It was while she lived in Cincinnati that she would observe the evils of slavery firsthand. Cincinnati was where she would marry and start her own family, and it was also where she would begin to write professionally.

While Catharine was the head of the Hartford Female Seminary and Harriet was a teacher, Lyman Beecher was trying to lead a religious revival in Boston. The people of Boston did not readily follow the strict Calvinism of Lyman Beecher, and they did not like his sermons on temperance, in which he spoke against the drinking of alcohol.

In 1830, the church where Lyman Beecher was a pastor caught fire. As the fire burned, jugs of rum that a liquor merchant had stored in the church basement without Lyman Beecher's knowledge exploded in the fire's

DEMOCRATIC TICKET.

FOR PRESIDENT,
MARTIN VAN BUREN.
FOR VICE PRESIDENT,
RICHARD M. JOHNSON.

OHIO ELECTORS.

JOHN M. GOODENOW,
OTHNIEL LOOKER,
JACOB FELTER,
JAMES B. CAMERON,
DAVID S. DAVIS,
JAMES FIFE,
JOHN J. HIGGINS,
JOSEPH MORRIS,
JAMES SHARP,
JOHN McELVAIN,
WILLIAM TREVITT,
DAVID ROBB,
HUGH McCOMB,
ROBERT MITCHELL,
JAMES MATHEWS,
JOSHUA SENEY,
STEPHEN N. SARGENT,
THOMAS J. McLAIN,
NOAH FREDERICK,
JACOB IHRIG,
JAMES MEANS.

This voter's guide from the 1836 election urges Ohio's citizens to cast their ballots for Democratic candidates. The campaign slogan "Going the Whole Hog" capitalizes on one of Ohio's' major industries.

Another name for Cincinnati was Porkopolis, because Cincinnati was near many large hog farms and had a port on a major river. Many hogs were brought to the town for slaughter and then were shipped to other towns and cities for sale. A large amount of Cincinnati's business was related to pork, and pigs often roamed the streets. They frequently ate the garbage that the residents left outside. In an 1832 letter to her sister, Harriet wrote of her young half brother, "We saw him parading by the house with his arm over the neck of a great hog, apparently on the most amicable terms possible." Although the sight of her brother embracing a pig in the street was entertaining, pig manure, garbage on the streets, and a lack of proper drainage meant that Cincinnati was subject to outbreaks of disease.

heat. This incident embarrassed Lyman Beecher. It was at this time that he realized that he was not popular in Boston.

With this in mind, when Lyman Beecher was invited to become the head of Lane Theological Seminary, he took the job. Lane Seminary was located in Walnut Hills, just outside of Cincinnati, Ohio. In March 1832, he and Catharine went west to Cincinnati to explore the prospect of living there. At the time, Cincinnati was a growing metropolis on America's frontier.

This engraving, which is one of four panels, was designed and published by J. W. Barber in 1826. The title is *The Drunkard's Progress, or The Direct Road to Poverty, Wretchedness & Ruin*. Shown here is the third panel, *The Confirmed Drunkard*. The temperance movement informed the public of the many problems caused by drinking alcohol.

While Catharine traveled with her father, Harriet was left to run the Hartford Female Seminary. Harriet exhausted herself in her new duties, but Lyman Beecher soon asked all his family to join him and Catharine in Cincinnati. Catharine also wanted Harriet to help her found and run a female academy in Cincinnati like the one Catharine had founded in Hartford.

Although Catharine hired several men with experience running schools to head the Hartford Female Seminary after she and Harriet left, the number of students at the school soon declined. The salaries necessary to pay married men with families to support were greater than the salaries of single, female teachers. As a result the teaching staff and the subjects offered at the school were cut back.

In October 1832, the Beechers came from Boston and Hartford and gathered in New York to move west

When Henry Ward Beecher heard that his father might move the family west to Cincinnati he was thrilled: "I sang, whistled, flew round like a mad man. Father's removal to the West is my 'hearts desire.'" This painting of Cincinnati was done in 1837.

to Cincinnati. Lyman Beecher saw the move as an opportunity to spread his brand of Christian religion across an expanding America. Harriet was less interested in spreading religion. She was more interested in leaving the familiar lands of Connecticut and New England to observe the diverse and rapidly expanding American West. Harriet was twenty-one years old at this time.

Estimates of Cincinnati's population show that it exploded from 10,000 in 1820 to 114,000 in 1851. When the Beecher family arrived in Cincinnati in the 1830s, the population was about 25,000 and growing. Known as the Queen City, Cincinnati already had many hotels, libraries, and theaters. Cincinnati's location on the Ohio River provided easy access for farmers to transport crops and animals, and for merchants to trade with other cities. Cincinnati was also right across the river from Kentucky, a slaveholding state. Part of Cincinnati's growth occurred because it was near the large farms in Kentucky that used slave labor.

Once she was situated in Cincinnati, Harriet helped Catharine to set up her new school, the Western Female Institute. For Harriet, the work at the new school was very demanding. She worked for many hours, but it was not as rewarding for her as it was for her sister. Harriet Beecher was not sure if she wanted to be a school-teacher for the rest of her life. In 1833, she wrote to Georgiana May, "My whole time has been taken up in

Pictured here, from left to right, is the faculty of Lane Theological
Seminary: Calvin Stowe, future husband to Harriet and professor
of biblical literature; Lyman Beecher, president of the seminary;
and Diarca H. Allen, another professor. By the tenth anniversary
of the school's opening, the seminary had taught 256 young men.

the labor of our new school, or wasted in the fatigue and lassitude following such labor." Harriet was depressed, and she mentioned that she had been having "illness and bad feelings of divers kinds."

Because they published a book on geography and founded a school for young women, Harriet and Catharine were invited to join the Semi-Colon Club. In this literary club, members prepared articles, letters, and poems to be read at the meetings, which were usually held in the parlor of a member's home. At this time in America, many educated and wealthy people socialized in literary clubs. They would gather to discuss literature, politics, and current events. Harriet's participation in Cincinnati's literary circles brought her great pleasure.

The Semi-Colon Club provided Harriet with the opportunity to meet many new people. One such couple was Eliza Tyler Stowe and Calvin Stowe. Calvin Stowe was a

Harriet and Eliza Tyler Stowe, Calvin's first wife, were close friends and shared many similar interests. This oil painting of Eliza by Hoyt was done around 1852.

respected biblical scholar who had recently begun teaching at Lane Seminary, of which Lyman Beecher was president. Eliza was a smart, educated woman with whom Harriet immediately became friends.

Harriet Beecher's letters and writings were well received by the Semi-Colon Club. One member was the publisher of the *Western Monthly Magazine*, and he suggested that Harriet submit some of her works. In 1834, one of her articles, a character sketch called "Uncle Lot," won a contest that the magazine had sponsored.

For the Semi-Colon Club and in her letters, Harriet wrote descriptions of scenes, or sketches, that described an event, a person, or an activity in detail. At the club, she could see how the members reacted to her writing, and she adjusted her work so that she could get the reaction that she wanted. Harriet also practiced writing in a colloquial voice, or writing the way characters would actually talk. She would use this experience of writing vivid descriptions and writing in local dialects in her later work.

5. Wife, Mother, and Writer

This introduction to literary society allowed Harriet to move away from her career as a schoolteacher and begin writing more for an audience. Harriet soon earned money from her writing.

In 1834, Harriet Beecher went back east to attend her brother Henry Ward Beecher's graduation from Amherst College. During this time, there was an outbreak of cholera, a contagious and deadly disease, in Cincinnati. One of the victims of the epidemic was Eliza Tyler Stowe, Harriet's friend. When she returned to Cincinnati, Harriet and the Beecher family comforted Calvin Stowe for his loss.

Harriet Beecher's friendship with Calvin Stowe soon bloomed into something more. They began to attend activities together, such as the Semi-Colon Club meetings. In January 1836, Calvin Stowe and Harriet Beecher were married. Soon after their marriage, Harriet Beecher Stowe became pregnant. Calvin Stowe was asked by the state of Ohio to go to Prussia, which is part of Germany today, to study their school system.

PRUSSIA

Scale of English Statute Miles

The couple considered whether Harriet should also make the long trip, but Calvin Stowe left on his own in June 1836, just a few months after being married. Calvin would remain abroad for approximately eight months. In the fall of 1836, while Calvin was in Europe, Harriet Beecher Stowe gave birth to twin girls. She named them Eliza and Harriet.

During the next fourteen years, Harriet had seven children in total. Six of them were born in Cincinnati, and the last was born in Brunswick, Maine. Henry Ellis Stowe was born in 1838, Frederick William Stowe was born in 1840, Georgiana May Stowe was born in 1843, Samuel Charles Stowe was born in 1848, and Charles Edward Stowe was born in 1850. Frequent childbirth left Harriet Beecher Stowe ill for long periods of time.

The twins, Eliza and Harriet Stowe, remained close all their lives. They are shown here in the 1860s disguised as clowns.

Opposite: This map of Prussia was engraved by John Dower and published by Orr and Smith in W. M. Higgins's *General Descriptive Atlas of the Earth* in 1836. Harriet wrote Calvin several notes before he set sail for Europe. A note was to be opened each week to remind Calvin of Harriet during his long voyage.

In 1836, Harriet Beecher Stowe quickly transformed from schoolteacher and single woman to wife and mother. Letters between members of the Beecher family and Harriet confirm Harriet's delight in the additions to the family, but surprise at the swift changes in her life. As a mother of newborn twins, Harriet did not sleep much, but she reported to her family that she was quite happy. She would not lead the life of a normal mother and wife, though. The domestic life that Harriet led was different from other women's lives at that time, because Harriet earned money from her writing and contributed to the family income.

Extra income was needed because Lane Seminary, where Calvin Stowe was a teacher, did not have a lot of money to pay its employees. A financial panic swept the country in 1837, and financial depression came to Cincinnati and other western cities in particular. Lane Seminary could not provide Calvin Stowe with the house he was promised as part of his pay. Harriet and Calvin had been looking forward to moving into a larger house with more space now that they had a family.

Campus debates on slavery and religion worked to decrease the number of students at Lane Seminary in the 1840s. The trustees, or people who controlled the money given to Lane Seminary, were wealthy because of their ties to slavery. Many trustees were merchants who bought, sold, or shipped crops from the large plantations in the South, and they had much to lose if slaves did not plant and harvest the crops. They did not want either the students or the teachers at Lane Seminary supporting or talking about freedom for slaves. Students who were abolitionists, or who believed that slaves should be freed immediately, left Lane Seminary for a rival school.

The effect was that Calvin Stowe's annual salary was just $600 at one point, down from more than $1,000 in the early 1830s. At the end of 1838, Harriet wrote, "We are rather better in that we now know exactly the state of our accounts—We are in debt."

Harriet Beecher Stowe had already determined what to do. "If you see my name coming out everywhere, you may be sure of one thing, that I do it for the pay," Harriet wrote to her friend Mary Dutton in 1838. To supplement the family income, Harriet Beecher Stowe wrote articles for money. Writing these articles provided Harriet with experience in writing for different audiences.

In 1833 and 1834, Harriet published five stories in the *Western Monthly Magazine*. This journal was for people in the expanding West of the United States. It gave readers a view of the way people lived and thought outside of New England. Articles in the *New-York Evangelist* were targeted toward a Christian audience and allowed Harriet to write sermons on such topics as temperance, religion, and salvation.

In 1839, Harriet Beecher Stowe began writing for *Godey's Lady's Book* and published eight stories and articles between 1839 and 1841. She was paid $15 per page for her work. The magazine was written for women, and Harriet supplied stories that promoted the influence of women just as women were taking a larger role in society.

Her first story for *Godey's Lady's Book* was "Trials of a Housekeeper," in which she detailed a woman's experience as a housekeeper. Harriet had always had servants around when she was growing up, and when she began her own family, she employed servants of her own. After the birth of the twins in 1836, and with the growing demands of her career as a writer, Harriet relied heavily on Anna Smith, her housekeeper.

Although Calvin Stowe supported Harriet with his encouraging words, she could not depend on him to help

Godey's Lady's Book proudly offered work by American writers to its reading audience. Most magazines relied on material previously published in British journals. *Godey's* also contained fashion plates, illustrating the latest trends in dresses and hats.

Calvin Stowe believed that Harriet could, and should, influence American society through her writing, "God has written it in his book, that you must be a literary woman, and who are we that we should contend against God?" This photograph of the couple was taken around 1850.

around the house because he was busy with his work as a teacher and a scholar. He was also unable to help out because he often did not feel well or claimed to have diseases that he did not actually have. Calvin was, however, a devoted father. He frequently played with the children, fed them, and took them for long walks.

Calvin championed Harriet's work as an author. In 1842, a publishing company offered to publish a collection of Harriet's work. Calvin wrote to his wife, "You must be a literary woman. . . . Make all your calculations accordingly, get a good stock of health, brush up your mind, drop the E out of your name, which only encumbers it and stops the flow . . . and write yourself only and always, Harriet Beecher Stowe."

In 1843, Harriet's collection of stories *The Mayflower; or, Sketches of Scenes and Characters among the Descendants of the Pilgrims* was published. This accomplishment was overshadowed by the death of Harriet's brother George. In addition, the Stowes still had financial troubles, and Harriet's health continued to be poor after the birth of Georgiana May. Harriet felt extremely weak and suffered from frequent headaches.

The suicide, sickness, and financial troubles made Harriet depressed. In 1845, she wrote to Calvin Stowe, "It is a dark, sloppy, rainy, muddy, disagreeable day, and I have been working hard (for me) all day in the kitchen, washing dishes, looking into closets, and seeing a great deal of that dark side of domestic life . . . I

This medicine kit belonged to Harriet Beecher Stowe. Doctors in the 1800s often prescribed blue pills called Calomel, which contained mercurous chloride. Harriet, along with countless others who took this drug, probably suffered from mercury poisoning. The symptoms included headaches, weakness in the hands, confusion, and irritability.

am sick of the smell of sour milk, and sour meat, and sour everything . . . and altogether I feel as if I never wanted to eat again."

With her mental and physical health in decline, Harriet spent fourteen months, starting in March 1846, at a water cure, or health spa, in Brattleboro, Vermont. Calvin and the family stayed in Cincinnati during Harriet's absence. At the spa, she soaked in baths and exercised, away from the stresses of raising so many children. This helped Harriet to relax, and restored her

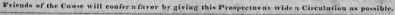

Friends of the Cause will confer a favor by giving this Prospectus as wide a Circulation as possible.

PROSPECTUS.

THE GREAT WANT OF THE AGE IS HEALTH—the normal and harmonious Action of all the Elements of our Being, Physical, Intellectual, Affectional, and Social. This Want finds its Satisfaction and this Demand its Supply in a Knowledge of the LAWS OF LIFE, or a true PHYSIOLOGY; the NATURE and CAUSES of DISEASE, or a true PATHOLOGY; the modes of PURIFICATION and INVIGORATION, or a TRUE SYSTEM of MEDICAL PRACTICE. These and kindred subjects, constituting

THE PHILOSOPHY OF HEALTH, and comprising the LAWS of PHYSICAL, MORAL and INTELLECTUAL DEVELOPMENT, are the especial sphere of the WATER-CURE JOURNAL; but all that can promote the great design of human happiness, may be included under its sub-title of HERALD OF REFORMS.

OUR PLATFORM is a broad one, and our Plan of Operations comprehensive. All subjects connected with Diet, Exercise, Cleanliness, Ventilation, Dwellings, Clothing, Education, Occupations, Amusements, and Social Relations—all the elements which combine to make that complex thing called Life, will be fully presented.

HYDROPATHY will be fully unfolded, and so explained that all may apply it in various diseases, even those not curable by any other means. The Water-Cure is not equaled by any other mode of treatment in those peculiar complaints commonly only to WOMEN. The WATER-CURE JOURNAL will contain such advice and instruction as may be considered most important in all these critical yet unavoidable cases.

THE

WATER-CURE JOURNAL

AND

HERALD OF REFORMS

FOR 1854.

DEVOTED TO PHYSIOLOGY, HYDROPATHY, AND THE LAWS OF LIFE.

TERMS, IN ADVANCE:

Single Copy, one year $1 00 | Ten Copies, one year $7 00
Five Copies, one year 4 00 | Twenty Copies, 1 year 10 00

Please address all letters, POST-PAID, to

FOWLERS AND WELLS,

Clinton Hall, 131 Nassau Street, New York.

VOLUME XVII.

PRESERVATION OF HEALTH.—Without HEALTH, even life is not desirable, unless a remedy can be found. It will be part of our duty to teach the world how to preserve health, as well as cure disease.

REFORMS in all our modes of life will be pointed out, and made so plain that "he who runs may read." We believe fully, that man may prolong his life much beyond the number of years usually attained. We propose to show how.

HOME TREATMENT.—Particular directions will be given for the treatment of ordinary cases at Home, which will enable all who have occasion to apply it without the aid of a Physician. Let it be borne in mind, that the WATER-CURE JOURNAL is a thoroughly POPULAR WORK, and not the Organ of a Profession or Sect.

THE FUTURE.—While the achievements of the PAST are the best promise of the FUTURE, we may intimate, that it is our intention to give in our own works, an example of the PROGRESS, REFORM, AND IMPROVEMENT, which we would promote in the most vital interests of men and of society.

TO THE FRIENDS OF HUMAN ELEVATION.—Believing the HEALTH REFORM to be the needed basis of all Reforms, and that no agency can be more efficient in promoting it than the WATER-CURE JOURNAL, we rely upon the FRIENDS of the CAUSE of HUMAN ELEVATION to continue their exertions until a copy is within the reach of EVERY FAMILY IN THE UNITED STATES.

THE JOURNAL will be published in a beautiful Quarto, for binding, on the first of each month.

Please be particular to write all names of persons and places plainly.

The Water Cure Journal and Herald of Reforms for 1854 educated readers on the science and techniques of the water cure. Harriet's regimen at the Brattleboro Water Cure included daily showers, baths, and the ingestion of many glasses of water. This hydropathy, or water cure, was to remove harmful substances from the body.

health. In 1848, as Calvin went off for his own water cure, Harriet gave birth to a healthy son, Samuel Charles Stowe.

Unfortunately, Samuel Charles, or Charley, died when he was eighteen months old, when another outbreak of cholera ravaged Cincinnati in 1849. The loss of young children was more common in the 1800s than it is today, but Harriet was deeply saddened. The emotions she felt after losing a child would figure strongly in the images she created in *Uncle Tom's Cabin*.

Memorial photos of the deceased were common in the nineteenth century. Samuel Charles Stowe, victim of an 1849 cholera epidemic, was photographed as if he had simply fallen asleep. Memorial photos, which were less expensive than paintings, allowed both the rich and the poor to have a lasting memento of a loved one.

Shortly after Charley's death, Calvin Stowe was offered a job teaching at Bowdoin College in Brunswick, Maine. At the end of 1849, Harriet Beecher Stowe was pregnant again, but she began the journey back to New England in April 1850 anyway. Her education as an author would soon be combined with a renewed energy brought about by her return to her native New England. This mixture would produce the most influential writing of her career.

6. Slavery and the Background to *Uncle Tom's Cabin*

The issue of slavery had been an important topic in Beecher family discussions because of the proximity of the family to slavery while they lived in Cincinnati. Lyman Beecher had also given antislavery sermons while the family lived in Litchfield, Connecticut. Harriet's experience in Cincinnati and her family's views would shape her own opinions on slavery. Her first visit to the South was around 1833, when she took a short trip to the home of a student on a plantation in Kentucky. She saw how hard the slaves worked in the fields and witnessed their poor living conditions.

Harriet learned about the institution of slavery by reading accounts of the harsh treatment of slaves through freedom narratives and abolitionist literature. Freedom narratives, which were also known as slave narratives, were stories told by former slaves that described the hard work and punishment that they faced in the South, as well as their escape to the North.

Harriet had also listened to the debates about slavery that were going on nationally and within her family.

These were the slave quarters on the Hermitage plantation in Savannah, Georgia. Slave quarters were cramped. An entire family might live inside one small room. Wooden shutters, rather than glass panes, closed the windows of slave quarters. The floors of these cabins were usually only the bare earth. Beds and bedding ranged from a wooden board to a mattress stuffed with straw to simply a pile of straw heaped upon the floor.

Back in 1834, the campus of Lane Seminary had held what came to be known as the Lane Debates. The students debated the two most popular ideas for ending slavery and then voted to support the immediate abolition of slavery.

The conservative position was to support the gradual emancipation and recolonization of slaves back in Africa. The more radical position was for the immediate abolition of slavery. It was the latter position that the students and many Beecher family members came to

The American Anti-Slavery Society produced these illustrations depicting the cruelty of slavery for its *Anti-Slavery Almanac for 1840*. The society was founded in 1833, with the goal of abolishing slavery in the United States. By 1840, there were approximately 200,000 members.

support. Lyman and Catharine Beecher held more conservative views, but William and George Beecher
moved toward the more radical views of immediate
abolition. The rest of the Beecher family would also
shift to a more radical antislavery view during the
next decade.

In 1837, the citizens of Cincinnati considered
whether to close down the press of the *Philanthropist*,
an abolitionist newspaper run by James Birney. Both
the debate over slavery and the issue of free speech
divided the town. Tensions rose during the summer of
1837, and the office of the *Philanthropist* was attacked
by a mob. Nine days later, a second mob formed and
there were riots in the streets of Cincinnati. The
paper's printing press was destroyed and thrown into
the river.

After these riots, Harriet wrote an anonymous edi-
torial on the right of free speech. Later she would
endorse the immediate abolition of slavery as well.
Another event that influenced Harriet occurred in
1839. Word came to Calvin Stowe that a black servant
who worked for the Stowe family was a runaway
slave, and the master was in town looking for her.
Rather than turning the slave over to the owner,
Calvin Stowe and Henry Ward Beecher took the
woman to a cabin that was a station on the
Underground Railroad. The Underground Railroad
was a series of safe houses and routes to the North

Thomas L. Gray is pictured in front of his home, which became a station, or safe house, on the Underground Railroad in Deavertown, Morgan County, Ohio. An escaped slave would receive a warm meal at a safe house and perhaps a night of rest. The slave would then head onto the next house on his or her long journey to freedom.

that allowed between sixty thousand and seventy-five thousand slaves to escape from slavery in the South.

The personal experiences that Harriet Beecher Stowe had with slavery and her siblings' support of abolition led Harriet to write "Immediate Emancipation" in 1845. This article was published in the *New-York Evangelist*, and it highlighted Harriet's belief that the institution of slavery had to be abolished because it was cruel and immoral. This short story described the hard life of a slave. Harriet used

Slavery was as old as the settlement of America itself, as the first slaves had arrived in Jamestown, Virginia, in 1619. Slave traders abducted or bartered for more than nine million slaves from Africa to work on the large cotton, rice, tobacco, and sugarcane plantations of North America and South America. Many African slaves who were packed tightly onto traders' ships died of disease and malnutrition on the trip to the Americas. In 1850, there were more than three million slaves in the United States, and most worked on cotton plantations in the South. Slaves were treated as property. They worked long hours doing backbreaking labor, and often suffered cruel punishment at the hands of slave owners.

regional dialects in the writing to achieve an authentic effect.

Tensions over the issue of slavery were high across the country in 1850, when Harriet was going from Cincinnati to Brunswick, Maine. One of the burning issues at the time was the Fugitive Slave Act, which was being debated in Congress at the time of Harriet's journey. The act was soon passed into law in September 1850. This law required people from the North to assist actively in returning escaped slaves to the South. It also removed what little legal protection was available to runaway

This 1850 lithograph by Theodor Kaufmann is called *Effects of the Fugitive-Slave Law.* The passage of the Fugitive Slave Law further divided the North and the South. Antislavery states passed additional state legislation that attempted to undo the new law.

slaves, and anyone who assisted runaway slaves could be fined $1,000 and sent to prison.

Immediately after the act was passed, accounts grew of blacks being kidnapped in the North and enslaved in the South. Harriet's correspondence with Henry Ward Beecher in New York, Isabella Beecher Hooker in Hartford, and Edward Beecher in Boston reinforced her view that the Fugitive Slave Law was wrong.

Charles Edward Stowe recalled that his mother, Harriet, received a letter from her sister-in-law Isabella P. Beecher that said, "If I could use a pen as you can, I would write something that would make this whole nation feel what an accursed thing slavery is." Charles recalled that Harriet stood up and said to her children, "I will write something. I will if I live."

At the beginning of 1851, Harriet Beecher Stowe began to create the stories that would become known as the novel *Uncle Tom's Cabin; or, Life Among the Lowly*. Harriet recalled that at a church service in early 1851, a vision came to her of a slave being brutally whipped. She went home and recorded the image from her vision in writing.

In March 1851, she wrote to Gamaliel Bailey, the editor of a moderate abolitionist paper called the *National Era*. Harriet proposed to write a series of stories that would run across three or four issues of the magazine, which would address the oppressive and immoral nature of slavery to a national audience.

In her letter to Bailey, she wrote that she would "hold up in the most lifelike and graphic manner possible Slavery, its reverses, changes, and the negro character, which I have had ample opportunities for studying." She also wrote that she would "show the best side of the thing, and something faintly approaching the worst."

Harriet Beecher Stowe knew that this series of sketches would be a large undertaking, but she had no idea that it would catapult her into the national debate on slavery and to international fame. She wrote to Bailey that before she had felt "no particular call to meddle with this subject," but that "the time is come when even a woman or a child who can speak a word for freedom and humanity is bound to speak."

7. Uncle Tom's Cabin

On June 5, 1851, the first part of *Uncle Tom's Cabin; or, Life Among the Lowly* appeared in the *National Era*. The series of stories would run until April 1, 1852. Many people around the nation closely followed Harriet Beecher Stowe's stories. When the stories were put together in a two-volume novel published in March 1852, her antislavery message reached a greater audience.

Uncle Tom's Cabin follows the lives of four slaves: Uncle Tom, George and Eliza, who are a couple, and their son, Harry. The hero of the novel, for the first time in American literature, was a slave, Uncle Tom. Tom is a strong, courageous man who endures his position as a slave to protect his children from being sold to another plantation and because of his strong Christian belief in God. When the story begins, Tom lives in a cabin on the Kentucky plantation of Mr. Shelby. Eliza and her baby son Harry are also slaves on Mr. Shelby's plantation. Mr. Shelby is a kind slaveholder, but he is having financial trouble. George, Harry's father, is a slave on the neighboring plantation of the cruel Mr. Harris.

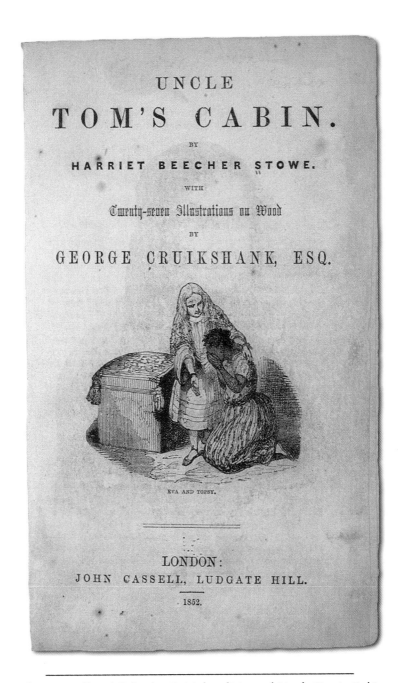

UNCLE
TOM'S CABIN.

BY

HARRIET BEECHER STOWE.

WITH

Twenty-seven Illustrations on Wood

BY

GEORGE CRUIKSHANK, ESQ.

EVA AND TOPSY.

LONDON:
JOHN CASSELL, LUDGATE HILL.

1852.

John Cassell published a British edition of *Uncle Tom's Cabin* in 1852. The book was popular in England, and Harriet obliged an abolitionist in London with information about herself. Stowe teasingly wrote, "I am a little bit of a woman—somewhat more than 40—about as thin & dry as a pinch of snuff. . . ."

After being whipped and beaten, George decides that he will run away to Canada and then buy the freedom of his wife and son. Soon after George leaves, Eliza finds out that Mr. Shelby, her owner, must sell her son, Harry, and Uncle Tom to a slave trader, Mr. Haley. That night, Eliza decides to escape in order to save her son and prevent him from being taken from her. The scene in which Eliza escapes across the river on blocks of ice while being pursued by Haley is one of the most memorable scenes in the book. It was based on a story of an actual slave escape about which Harriet had once been told.

This lithograph by Charles Bour was an illustration in the novel *Uncle Tom's Cabin*. The scene depicts Eliza's perilous flight across the ice with her child.

The slave trader, Mr. Haley, could not catch Eliza, who makes her way north and reunites with her husband, George. In the story, Harriet Beecher Stowe carefully portrays George and his family as human beings, not just as slaves. The courage that Eliza shows in her escape, and that George displays in a "declaration of independence" when slave traders later surround him, illustrated that enslaved black people were human. This sent a strong message at a time when most Americans thought of black people as property.

The day after Eliza's escape, Mr. Haley takes Uncle Tom down the Mississippi River to be sold. Along the way, a young girl named Eva falls into the mighty river and Tom jumps in and saves her. The girl's father, Augustine St. Clare, buys Tom from Mr. Haley because of his good deed. Augustine St. Clare is not a cruel slave owner, but he does not set Tom free.

Harriet attempted to depict some slave owners as good people who were victims of an evil system. Tom's time at the St. Clare plantation does not last, because Eva falls ill and dies, and Augustine St. Clare soon dies as well. Harriet used her own feelings about her son Charley and her grief over his death to express the love that Augustine St. Clare has for his daughter, Eva. In another scene, Mrs. Bird, a woman who is helping the

---

Next spread: A costume guide offers theatrical companies some suggestions on how to dress a character and create backdrops and scenery for a particular scene in a play. This is a plate from *Webb's Characters & Scenes in Uncle Tom's Cabin*, published around 1850.

George Harris 5th dress   Eliza

Dick Willis

Uncle Tom

Legree

George Harris 2d dress

Legree

Sambo

escaped slave Eliza, cries as she gives some clothes to Eliza's son, Harry. These garments belonged to Mrs. Bird's own son, who had died when he was young. Harriet's words created graphic images based on the pain that she had experienced.

After Augustine St. Clare's death, Tom is sold to Simon Legree, a cruel plantation owner. Legree beats and abuses Tom, but Tom tells Legree that he will never own Tom's soul. Harriet Beecher Stowe deliberately made Tom a Christlike figure. Tom keeps his faith despite all the persecution and abuse that he experiences. Later critics would blast the character of Tom as a product of Harriet's racism. Today an Uncle Tom is known as a black person who submits to pressure from whites or tries to act like a white person.

One of the other slaves on the Legree plantation is Cassy, who has also suffered from Legree's harsh treatment. When Cassy escapes, Legree takes out his anger on Tom, who will not reveal her hiding place. Tom is beaten and whipped to his death. Just before Tom dies, the son of his former owner, George Shelby, comes to buy Tom back. Tom is glad that he hasn't been forgotten. He asks George to take a loving, final message to Chloe, who is Tom's wife. George swears that he will always remember Tom. When George returns to Kentucky, he frees all his slaves and becomes an abolitionist.

Uncle Tom's Cabin combined a story of individual abuse and suffering with a condemnation of the

This is a portrait of publisher John P. Jewett. To boost the strong sales of *Uncle Tom's Cabin*, Jewett marketed a special holiday edition, which had one hundred engravings by well-known artists.

institution of slavery that spoke to many Americans. In March 1852, Harriet Beecher Stowe signed a contract with John P. Jewett, a Boston book publisher, to compile and publish *Uncle Tom's Cabin*. His initial offer was to split the profits if the Stowes could pay for half the cost of manufacturing the book. The Stowes could not afford to publish the book, so they were paid ten percent of the royalties of sales in the United States.

Uncle Tom's Cabin was a huge success. Three hundred thousand copies were sold in the first year that it was published, which earned the Stowes $10,000. Although Harriet missed out on a greater share of the profits, she was on her way to becoming the highest-paid author of her century. The book was also a best-seller in England and was eventually translated into more than sixty languages. Unfortunately, the Stowes did not receive any money from the international sales, but for the time being their financial situation improved.

Harriet was not the first person to write about the cruel treatment of slaves or the immorality of slavery. The success of her book was due to the way she was able to combine facts and fiction to tell her story. Much of her knowledge about slavery came from abolitionists and the written and oral accounts of former slaves. Literature of that time described the hard labor slaves were forced to do on the large plantations, and the brutal whippings they received if they could not continue to work.

When she got to the point in the story where Tom is sent to work on a plantation in the Deep South, Harriet turned to her brother Charles Beecher, who had worked in New Orleans, for information. Harriet's cook in Cincinnati, Eliza Buck, also told of her experiences as a slave in Virginia and Louisiana. Eliza recounted the sexual abuse and poor treatment slave women experienced at the hands of their masters.

Harriet also borrowed from the freedom narratives, also known as slave narratives, of Josiah Henson and Henry Bibb. These two former slaves wrote of their escape from slavery through a route in Cincinnati. Most freedom narratives described the escape of a male slave. *Uncle Tom's Cabin* featured the escape of a female slave.

Harriet also consulted the autobiography of Frederick Douglass. She even wrote Douglass a letter to request information, explaining that within her story, "The scene will fall upon a cotton plantation—I am very desirous to gain information from one who has been an actual labourer on one—& it occurred to me that in the circle of your acquaintances there might be one who would be able to communicate to me some such information."

As Harriet waited for this information, she missed the deadline for the *National Era*'s publication. Her research and other family issues would cause Harriet to miss the deadline for her series several times. When she missed a deadline, the editors of the *National Era* would include a note in the issue that the chapter was delayed.

Harriet Beecher Stowe also drew from the work of abolitionists in creating her novel. There were more than one thousand small antislavery societies in America at the time, and about 250,000 abolitionists working for the end of slavery. She found Theodore Weld's *American Slavery as It Is* particularly useful. This book presented documentary evidence of the laws used to enforce slavery. It also offered the details of court cases and the harsh punishments and poor living conditions of slaves in the South.

After the detailed and emotional antislavery novel *Uncle Tom's Cabin* was published, there was a deep and widespread reaction. Northerners were presented with a

Frederick Douglass was an escaped slave who used his talents as a writer and an orator to denounce slavery in the United States. This portrait of Douglass was created by Elisha Hammond around 1844. Douglass's autobiography *Narrative of the Life of Frederick Douglass, an American Slave* was published in 1845.

different view of slavery than the one they had previously seen, and they were outraged. In his biography of her, Charles Edward Stowe recorded the praise for his mother's book that came from famous Americans such as the poet Henry Wadsworth Longfellow who wrote, "It is one of the greatest triumphs recorded in literary history."

This praise also flowed in from across the ocean. Charles Dickens wrote, "I have read your book with the deepest sympathy and interest, and admire, more than I can express to you, both the generous feeling which inspired it, and the admirable power

Charles Edward Stowe, photographed around 1880, was a minister. When he wrote to his mother of problems with his parish in Maine, Harriet gave him this advice, "When things are so that you feel as if you couldn't hold on a minute longer—never give up then—for the tide is sure to turn."

with which it is executed." The British historian Thomas Macaulay said that it was "the most valuable addition that America has made to English literature."

People in America's South did not react positively to the book and were very defensive. They felt that Harriet Beecher Stowe could not know the South or slavery

UNCLE TOM'S CABIN

UNCLE TOM & EVA.

This 1899 lithograph, captioned "Uncle Tom & Eva," was a poster advertising a production of *Uncle Tom's Cabin*.

The popularity of Uncle Tom's Cabin led to the creation of games, toys, songs, poems, and plays based on the novel. Most of the plays based on the novel were not true to the original story and message of the book. They shortened the plot, eliminated the political discussions of abolition, and changed the character of Uncle Tom from a strong young man to an old, weak man. White actors played all the parts of black slaves by painting their faces black, which was common at the time if a black character was part of a play. Theater companies also added gimmicks to attract an audience, such as music. In some productions, live dogs chased Eliza in the scene where she escaped to freedom.

because she had not been there. They accused her of making up details or of focusing on a few extreme cases of slave abuse. Not only did newspaper reviewers for the *Atlanta Planter* and *New Orleans Crescent* attack the book as falsely portraying slavery, they also attacked Harriet Beecher Stowe as "wicked" or "monstrous." Some northerners also attacked the book, and northern members of the clergy felt that they had not been portrayed favorably.

To answer the critics, who accused her of knowing nothing about slavery, Stowe wrote *A Key to Uncle Tom's Cabin* in 1853. This book compiled the sources of her research and presented the facts and accounts that were combined with her religious antislavery message to make up the story of *Uncle Tom's Cabin*.

People in the South said slavery was necessary because blacks were inferior and would not be able to live on

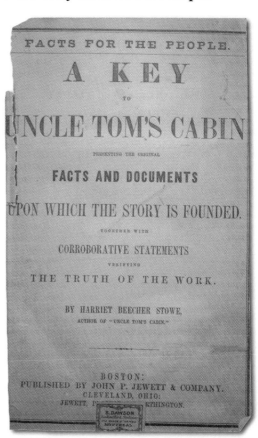

Stowe's factual accounting of the cruelties of slavery, *A Key to Uncle Tom's Cabin*, was criticized in the South as being unsuitable material for a woman author.

their own without supervision. Anti-Tom literature was written by proslavery advocates in the South who argued that slaves had kind masters and were treated better than were the free blacks in the North. Some of the books published in response to *Uncle Tom's Cabin* were *Aunt Phyllis's Cabin; or, Southern Life as It Is* and *Uncle Robin, in His Cabin in Virginia, and Tom Without One in Boston.*

The literature from the South also argued that the North had many poor black and white workers who suffered from low wages, long hours, and deadly working conditions in northern factories. The writing that the South published in support of slavery angered abolitionists, who rejected any arguments that endorsed slavery.

8. The Civil War

At the beginning of 1852, Calvin Stowe took a new job as a teacher at the Andover Theological Seminary, and the Stowe family moved to Andover, Massachusetts. *Uncle Tom's Cabin* was published as a book in March 1852. As it sold an increasing number of copies in the North, the South, and Europe, Harriet Beecher Stowe became a celebrity. When Harriet paid a visit to her brother Henry Ward Beecher in New York City, she attracted attention in the street and received free tickets to a sold-out Broadway play.

It was not just the people of the North who responded positively to *Uncle Tom's Cabin*. In 1853, the Antislavery Society of Glasgow, Scotland, invited Harriet to tour the British Isles. Calvin and Harriet left their children with Harriet's family and sailed across the ocean on March 30, 1853.

Next page: This 1862 map of Europe was published in London in *Fullarton's Royal Illustrated Atlas*. The countries that Harriet and Calvin visited on their 1853 tour of Europe have been highlighted: Scotland, England, France, Belgium, Switzerland, and Germany.

EUROPE

BY J. B. SWANSTON, EDINBURGH

Map Key

England	**Scotland**	France
Belgium	**Switzerland**	Germany
Blue	**Orange**	Yellow
Brown	**Green**	Pink

Mathew Brady photographed the Beecher family around 1859. Brady was an acclaimed nineteenth-century photographer. In 1845, he undertook an ongoing project to photograph his famous contemporaries. He also went on to document the Civil War through his photography.

Throughout her tour of Scotland and England, Harriet Beecher Stowe was received by wealthy and well-known people, but she was also recognized and approached by people of the working class. People of all classes had read her book. Harriet and Calvin would tour France, Belgium, Switzerland, and Germany before returning to America in the fall of 1853. Upon her return, Harriet committed her memories to paper. In 1854, the memoir of her trip, *Sunny Memories of Foreign Lands*, was published.

John Steuart Curry's painting *John Brown of Osawatomie*
depicts the militant abolitionist John Brown railing against
slavery in Kansas. Henry Ward Beecher, who also preached
against slavery in Kansas, is painted on the left, holding a Bible.
This tribute to Brown was done eighty years after his death.

While Harriet was away in Europe, tensions continued to rise in America over the issue of slavery. Fights and shootings between abolitionists and proslavery advocates grew more frequent. The question of whether the territory of Kansas would become a free state or a slave state caused frequent violence to erupt in that territory. For her part, Harriet let abolitionists meet in her home, and she contributed money that she had collected in Scotland and England toward the antislavery cause.

In May 1856, a band of abolitionists led by John Brown
killed a group of proslavery
settlers in Kansas. In that
same year, the antislavery senator from Massachusetts,
Charles Sumner, was brutally
beaten on the Senate floor by
Preston Brooks, the proslavery
senator from South Carolina.

In 1856, Harriet finished
writing *Dred: A Tale of the
Great Dismal Swamp*, a second
antislavery novel. The story
had initially been written with
a more moderate tone in which
a slave owner becomes the
hero of the story. This more
sympathetic view of slave owners disappeared as the events
of 1856 unfolded. The main
character became Dred, a slave
who planned a rebellion similar to the slave rebellion led by
Nat Turner in 1830. Nat
Turner was a slave who orga-
nized a revolt in which he and
a group of slaves killed several slave owners on their

Henry Ward Beecher collected money
from his church to purchase Sharps
carbine rifles for abolitionist settlers
in Kansas. The rifles were shipped in
crates marked "Bibles" and became
known as Beecher's Bibles.

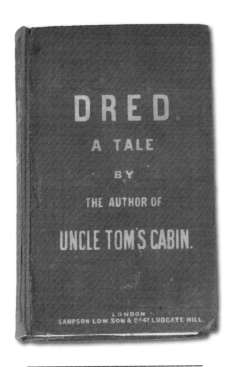

Brisk sales of *Dred* made up for the mixed reviews of critics. Harriet wrote Calvin, "One hundred thousand copies of 'Dred' sold in four weeks! After that who cares what the critics say?"

farms. In her novel, an evil slave owner shoots and kills Dred before he can take part in a rebellion.

The change in Harriet's attitude as she wrote the book hurt the quality of the plot and of the character development. Although the critics did not think it was a good follow-up to *Uncle Tom's Cabin*, the book still sold well. The book may have received additional attention because of the 1857 Supreme Court case *Dred Scott v. Sanford*. A slave named Dred Scott tried to use the legal system to win his freedom, but the Supreme Court decision declared that blacks could not file court cases because they were not citizens. This case also ruled that Congress could not pass laws against slavery in U.S. territories.

Toward the middle of 1856, Harriet Beecher Stowe made another trip to England, where she applied for a copyright for her new novel. After realizing how much money she had lost by not having a British copyright for *Uncle Tom's Cabin*, she worked to make sure that she had one filed in London for her other books. Soon after she returned, Harriet faced a personal crisis. In the summer of 1857, Henry Ellis Stowe, Harriet's oldest son and a student at Dartmouth, drowned in an accident on the Connecticut River. His death devastated Harriet and Calvin.

The events in her personal life and in the United States did not stop Harriet's work as a writer. She began writing articles for the

Harriet wrote the eulogy for Henry's funeral. After his death, Harriet visited Dartmouth, the college that Henry had attended. This portrait of Henry was taken around 1852.

Atlantic Monthly when this influential magazine was just starting out. Some of these articles were chapters of Harriet's newest novel, *The Minister's Wooing*.

The novel was set in Newport, Rhode Island, in the 1790s and focused on Calvinism as a religion. On one level, Harriet Beecher Stowe was writing about her New England heritage and her experiences with Calvinism. On a more radical and important level, Harriet was writing about the imperfections that she saw in Calvinist beliefs, and especially in the ministers who practiced them.

Harriet used a similar formula to that of *Uncle Tom's Cabin* in that she made the "lowly," or poorer, people the heroes of the novel. She pointed out that the ministers and theologians of the privileged class are more concerned with the philosophy or beliefs of their religion than they are about being compassionate. Writing after the death of her son Henry, Harriet suggested it is women who deal with pain and suffering. In *The Minister's Wooing*, the women and the poor people actually comfort others, not the ministers.

When the novel was published in 1859, Harriet made another trip to Europe to secure the copyrights for her newest book. At the same time, the United States was heading toward the Civil War. In 1859, the abolitionist John Brown led a raid on the arsenal at Harpers Ferry. Raiding a federal arsenal was considered treason. John Brown was captured, tried in court for treason, found to be guilty by a jury, and then hanged. As did many abolitionists, Harriet considered Brown a hero.

After Abraham Lincoln was elected president of the United States in November 1860, South Carolina seceded, or officially withdrew, from the United States on December 20. Alabama, Florida, Georgia, Louisiana, Mississippi, and Texas also seceded, and on February 18, 1861, Jefferson Davis was elected president of the Confederate States of America.

Frederick Stowe, photographed around 1861, dropped out of medical school to enlist in the army. Harriet anxiously wrote, "I know not what day the news may come to my house which has come to so many noble families of one more empty saddle & broken sword."

Harriet's son Frederick Stowe was a soldier in the Union army. He was an abolitionist who had enlisted in the army early in the war. In 1863, he was seriously injured at the Battle of Gettysburg. Frederick Stowe had been a heavy drinker before the war. The trauma of battle, his slow recovery from injury, and the morphine he used as a painkiller led Frederick Stowe back into alcoholism. Although Harriet tried many times to help Fred overcome his problem, he was never able to give up drinking. In 1871, Fred disappeared in California after traveling there to make a fresh start in his life.

Harriet Beecher Stowe met with President Abraham Lincoln in 1862. The purpose of her meeting was to lobby for the Emancipation Proclamation, which freed the slaves in the rebellious South. Lincoln signed the Emancipation Proclamation on New Year's Day in 1863. Harry Everett Townsend dramatized this event in his painting.

On April 12, 1861, the Confederate army attacked Fort Sumter in South Carolina and the Civil War began. Lincoln's original plan was to crush the armed rebellion in the Southern states within a few months and bring them back into the Union. The emancipation of all slaves was not part of this plan, and Harriet publicly criticized the president for not including it. In 1862, she met with Lincoln, and he was said to have remarked, "So you are the little lady who wrote the book that started this great war!"

The Confederate army put up fierce resistance to the Union army, and the war dragged on longer than anyone

This Civil War–era lithograph, *The Battle of Gettysburg, Pa. July 3d. 1863*, was published by Currier & Ives. The famous, three-day Battle of Gettysburg resulted in 51,000 casualties.

had expected. The Civil War would take more American lives than any war in American history. At the end of 1862, Lincoln decided that the emancipation of slaves would help him to bolster support in the North, win more foreign allies, and provide fresh soldiers in the form of former slaves.

The Emancipation Proclamation was signed at the beginning of 1863, to the great joy of Harriet and of the abolitionists in the North. The Civil War did not end until April 1865, when General Robert E. Lee of the Confederate army surrendered to General Ulysses S. Grant of the Union army. Congress passed the Thirteenth Amendment to the U.S. Constitution, which outlawed slavery, in December 1865. Black people still faced many challenges and hardships, but the institution of slavery was finally abolished.

9. Later Writings and the Movement for Women's Rights

Both during and after the Civil War, Harriet Beecher Stowe continued to write. She produced new novels and articles until 1878. At a time when the struggle for women's rights was gaining followers, Harriet was a prime example of what women could achieve.

In 1862, both *Agnes of Sorrento* and *The Pearl of Orr's Island* were published as novels. Like many of Stowe's novels, *Agnes of Sorrento* was written in installments and published by a magazine. *The Atlantic Monthly* began publishing the chapters, which were based on Harriet's recent travels to Italy, in 1861. The novel was not well constructed and was often overly romantic or sentimental, but it sold more than four hundred thousand copies.

Harriet also promised the antislavery newspaper *Independent* that she would write a story for them. She wrote the first chapters of *The Pearl of Orr's Island*, but after the start of the Civil War in April 1862, she was overwhelmed by trying to meet multiple deadlines. She quickly ended *The Pearl of Orr's Island* without fully developing either the plot or the ending of the story.

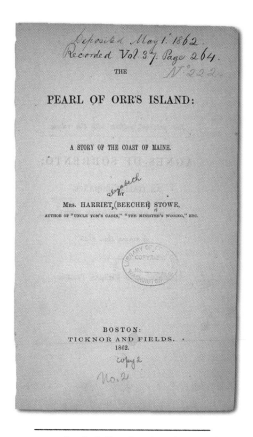

Harriet had difficulty finishing *The Pearl of Orr's Island* and wrote her editor, "Who could write stories, that had a son to send to battle, with Washington beleaguered, and the whole country shaken as with an earthquake?"

The Pearl of Orr's Island is set in Maine and focuses on the coming of age of a young woman at a time in America when there were few opportunities for women. The psychological struggles of this young woman as she grows up are based on similar struggles that Harriet faced as she finished her education and discovered that there were limited opportunities for women outside of the home. Some critics today feel that parts of the book are very good, and that, if Harriet had been able to finish the novel, it would have been considered a great book.

After 1863, Harriet had to write rather quickly, and she sacrificed more quality than she would have liked. That year, at age sixty-one, Calvin Stowe retired as a professor from Andover Theological Seminary. This meant that Harriet would have to support the family without the additional income provided by her husband's $2,000-per-year salary. She needed to make up this lost income by increasing the quantity of material that she wrote.

Her next set of articles, the "House and Home Papers," appeared in the pages of the *Atlantic Monthly* in 1864. Harriet created the character and homeowner Christopher Crowfield to write about subjects such as housekeepers, parlors, carpets, and other house-related issues. She hoped that these articles would provide comfort to her readers as the fighting of the Civil War dragged on.

She also published the "Chimney-Corner" articles in the *Atlantic Monthly* in 1865 and 1866. These articles were parables, in

Despite the substantial money she earned through her writing, Harriet often had to overextend herself to meet new financial obligations. In 1863, at the height of the Civil War, the Stowe family began construction on a house in Hartford, Connecticut. The house was called Oakholm and was the home that Harriet had always wanted. Oakholm was expensive to build and maintain, and the Stowes were later forced to sell their dream house.

which Stowe describes a brief domestic scene to make a point on topics such as repression, irritability, and intolerance. The following year, she wrote *Men of Our Times*, a series of short biographies on men such as Abraham Lincoln, Ulysses S. Grant, and Frederick Douglass. A similar proposal to write biographies of women did not result in a book because the publisher would not pay Harriet enough money for her work on these profiles.

Calvin Stowe had encouraged his wife to be a "literary woman" and consistently supported Harriet's efforts, but at times it was hard for him. "I suffer & have nothing," he wrote to Harriet. Harriet's work, Calvin wrote, brought her "living immortal children, Uncle Tom & Dred."

Now retired, Calvin Stowe was able to concentrate on a study of the Bible's New Testament that he'd begun writing back in 1835. Harriet encouraged him to work on his book, and she also wrote to her publishers asking them to consider buying Calvin's work. In 1867, *The Origin and History of the Books of the Bible* was published. The book was well received, and Calvin traveled to Harvard College and other institutions to lecture on his work.

The following year, 1868, Calvin and Harriet purchased a piece of land and built a second home in Mandarin, Florida. They had visited the state during the previous year, when they'd loaned their son Fred

Harriet, Calvin, one of their daughters, and a niece are seated on the porch of their house in Mandarin, Florida, around 1874. Photographers, tourists, and fans frequently dropped by to gawk at the famous writer.

money to rent and cultivate a plantation. Although Fred was initially able to stop his drinking, he eventually slipped back into alcoholism. Despite their son's condition, the Stowes enjoyed Florida's climate and found it a welcome change from the cold New England winters.

From 1868 until Calvin and Harriet could no longer make the trip for health reasons, the couple spent their winters in Florida. During their first winter in Florida, Harriet worked on another novel. *Oldtown Folks* was completed without first being serialized chapter by chapter in a magazine or a paper.

The novel was heavily based on stories from Calvin Stowe's childhood in Natick, Massachusetts, and Harriet's own New England upbringing. Critics felt the novel was longer than it needed to be and was too sentimental. A review in an influential newspaper, the *Nation*, was critical of the book. Harriet defended her book but also took offense at the fact that the *Nation* did not often give books by women good reviews. They admired men's novels, but labeled women's novels as too sentimental or romantic. Harriet publicly praised women's novels that she thought were good.

Harriet Beecher Stowe was not afraid either of controversy or of challenging what the critics said. At age sixty, Harriet came to the defense of her friend Lady Byron, whose character was being damaged in the press. Unlike *Uncle Tom's Cabin*, which had made Harriet a hero, her defense of Lady Byron almost

Anne Isabella Milbanke married Lord Byron in January 1815 and became Lady Byron. She separated from her husband one year later and went to live with her parents. This portrait of Lady Byron was done in the 1830s.

ruined her reputation. Harriet had first met Lady Byron, the widow of the romantic poet Lord George Gordon Byron, on her first trip to England in 1853. The friendship of Harriet Beecher Stowe and Lady Byron would last for many years.

During Harriet's trip to England in 1856, she spent time with Lady Byron before she died and learned that the famous poet Lord Byron treated Lady Byron badly and did not respect their marriage vows. It was solely Lord Byron's behavior and lifestyle that had led to the couple's separation. When a story by one of Lord Byron's friends blamed Lady Byron for Lord Byron's unhappiness and exile, Harriet felt it her duty to defend Lady Byron by publishing the truth about Lord Byron.

Awful Revelations in Regard to Shakespeare.

A most interesting and important revelation has just been made of the life of Shakespeare, by which the character of that depraved writer and most infamous man will come at last to be properly understood.

Shakespeare was not only the most prolific author of demoralizing plays, calculated to corrupt the youth of his own age and all succeeding ages (through the dramatic merit, nay, unquestionable genius, these plays unhappily exhibited)—he was a homicide, a Thug of the period, a man habitually given to murder, and led by this baleful proclivity to the deeper guilt of constantly maltreating Mrs. Shakespeare and keeping late hours with pot-house companions.

These facts have transpired at this late period, by reason of the discovery of an old manuscript, in the family of the Cherstows, giving the substance of conversations between one Mrs. H. B. Cherstow and Mrs. Shakespeare, a short time before the death of the latter. The manuscript has been published by Loring, of Boston, in a compact pamphlet, which will be generally accepted as one of the most valuable contributions ever made to English literary history.

Mrs. Shakespeare was induced to withdraw the veil from the blackness of her husband's character chiefly that the fatal effect of his writings, which had already begun to wane in popularity, might be forever therefore negatived. When the English people came to see him in his true colors, they would no longer tolerate his literary remains either in the library or on the stage.

The malevolent playwright, it seems, was accustomed to allure the authors of inferior dramas, whose plots he had stolen and immortalized, into the neighborhood of Stratford and there slay them, burying the bodies under a crab tree or a mulberry tree, which he sometimes called an elder tree, as convenience suited. His daughter was his fiendish accomplice in this work, and his wife was fully acquainted with the facts, but neither exposed them in Mr. Shakespeare's lifetime, nor abandoned her red-handed lord, with whom, however, her subsequent life of thirty-one years was one convulsive struggle with "a divided duty."

The terrible tragedies of Shakespeare, indeed the whole of his immoral writings, have a new significance when read by the light of these astounding developments. A hundred passages of the direst remorse will occur to any reader acquainted with the great, guilty dramatist, in which it is clear that his mind was dwelling upon the fearful details of his murderous career. Indeed, Mrs. Shakespeare and Mrs. H. B. Cherstow, her friend, were painfully impressed by a suspicion that this gifted mind was at times unhinged.

The old manuscript recites the curious circumstances under which Mrs. Shakespeare came to confide to Mrs. Cherstow the dreadful secret—how Mrs. S. sent for her—how she (Mrs. H. B. C.) went to Stratford—how, having taken a memorandum of the interview to London, she asked for time to consider the propriety of making it known to the world, and advised rather waiting until everybody who could deny the statement should be dead, &c., &c.

But enough. Let all who feel interested in having Shakespeare consigned to everlasting infamy buy the pamphlet, which may be obtained of any news agent for ten cents, and "sup full of horrors."

"LADY BYRON VINDICATED."

Mrs. Stowe's Defence of Her Story and Herself.

All Her "Facts" and "Proofs" Now Given.

Why the Story was not Sooner Made Public.

A FRESH ACCOUNT OF THE INTERVIEW.

Old Scandals, Letters, Reports and Rumors Revived and Reiterated.

Mrs. Stowe's *Lady Byron Vindicated*—her long-promised defence of her Byron scandal, published in the *Atlantic Monthly* last September—with all the facts and proofs in her possession, is announced for publication to-morrow. From advance sheets we are enabled to give the readers of the Times a summary of the book—a volume of nearly 500 pages—and copious extracts from it. It is divided into three parts. The first contains five chapters respectively entitled "Introduction," (which has already been printed in the Times;) "The Attack on Lady Byron;" "Résumé of the Conspiracy;" "Results After Lord Byron's Death;" and "The Attack on Lady Byron's Grave." The second, eight chapters: "Lady Byron as I Knew Her;" "Lady Byron's Story as Told to Me;" "Chronological Summary of Events;" "The Character of the two Witnesses Compared;" "The Direct Argument to Prove the Crime;" "Physiological Argument;" "How Could She Love Him;" and "Conclusion." And the third, miscellaneous documents for reference.

Part First may be dismissed in a paragraph, it being simply a *résumé* of the controversy regarding the character of Lord and Lady Byron since the separation. In attempting to prove what she has asserted, Mrs. Stowe makes four points: "1. A concerted attack upon Lady Byron's reputation, begun by Lord Byron in self-defence. 2. That he transmitted his story to friends to be continued after his death. 3. That they did so continue it. 4. That the accusations reached their climax over Lady Byron's grave in *Blackwood* of 1869, and the Guiccioli book, and that this reopening of the controversy was reason for speaking." Mrs. Stowe here brings forward no new evidence, but uses the *Academy* letter, the article in *Blackwood* of July, 1869, several of Byron's poems and letters, the report of an interview with Mrs. Minns, formerly Lady Byron's waiting-maid and now living, and the well-remembered letter, transmitted to the London *Times* by Lord Lindsay, from Lady Byron to Lady Anne Barnard.

Lady Byron as Mrs. Stowe Knew Her.

It is in the second part that Lady Byron is vindicated as far as Mrs. Stowe's ability goes. Mrs. Stowe says that Lady Byron's story was told her in language "clear, precise, terrible." But she did not produce her phrases and sentences word for word in her original *Atlantic Monthly* article, for two reasons: The public honor and incredulity would have been doubled, and she deemed it necessary that the brutality of the story should, in some degree, be veiled and softened. But now she feels that the tale must be told to the bitter end. She prefaces the narrative with some account of Lady Byron as she was during the time of their mutual acquaintance and friendship, "as the credibility of a history depends greatly on the character of its narrator, and as especial pains have been taken to destroy the belief in this story by representing it to be the wanderings of a broken-down mind in a state of dotage and mental hallucination."

LADY BYRON AT SIXTY-ONE.

Lord Byron has given in his journal a picture of Lady Byron at twenty, after her first refusal of him. "She is a poetess, a mathematician, a metaphysician; yet withal very kind, generous and gentle, with very little pretension. Any other head would be turned with half her acquisitions and a tenth of her advantages." Mrs. Stowe says she formed her acquaintance in 1853, in England. She met her at a lunch party. She was at this time sixty-one. To quote:

"Her form was slight, giving an impression of fragility; her motions were both graceful and decided; her eyes bright, and full of interest and quick observation. Her silvery-white hair seemed to lend a grace to the transparent purity of her complexion, and her small hands had a pearly whiteness. I recollect she wore a plain widow's cap, of a transparent material, and was dressed in some delicate shade of lavender, which harmonized well with her complexion. When I was introduced to her, I felt in a moment the words of her husband:

'There was awe in the homage that she drew;
Her spirit seemed as seated on a throne.'

Calm, self-poised, and thoughtful, she seemed to me rather to resemble an interested spectator of the world's affairs, than an actor involved in its trials; yet the sweetness of her smile, and a certain very delicate sense of humor in her remarks, made the way of acquaintance easy. Her first remarks were a little playful; but, in a few moments, we were speaking on what every one in those days was talking to me about—the slavery question in America. Lady Byron's remarks caught my ear, and arrested my attention by their peculiar incisive quality, their originality, and the evidence they gave that she was as well informed on all our matters as the best American statesman could be. I had no wearisome course to go over with her as to the difference between the General Government and State Governments, nor explanations of the United States Constitution; for she had the whole before her mind with a perfect clearness. Her morality upon the slavery question, too, impressed me as something far higher and deeper than the common sentimentalism of the day. Many of her words surprised me greatly, and gave me new material for thought.

I found I was in company with a commanding mind, and hastened to gain instruction from her on another point where my interest had been aroused. I found that she had studied with careful thoughtfulness all the social and religious tendencies of England during her generation. One of her remarks has often since occurred to me. Speaking of the Oxford movement, she said the time had come when the English Church could no longer remain as it was. It must either restore the past or create a future. The Oxford movement attempted the former; and of the future she was beginning to speak when our conversation was interrupted by the presentation of other parties. Subsequently, in reply to a note from her on some benevolent business, I alluded to that conversation, and expressed a wish that she would finish giving me her views of the religious state of England. A portion of the letter that she wrote me in reply I insert, as being very characteristic in many respects:

Various causes have been assigned for the decaying state of the English Church; which seems the more strange, because the clergy have improved, morally and intellectually, in the last twenty years. Then why should their influence be diminished? I think it is owing to the diffusion of a spirit of free inquiry.

Doubts have arisen in the minds of many who are unhappily bound by subscription not to doubt; and, in consequence, they are habitually pretending either to believe or to disbelieve. The state of Denmark cannot but be rotten, when to seem is the first object of the witnesses of truth.

They may lead better lives and bring forward abler arguments; but their efforts are paraly[illegible] by that unsoundness. I see the High Churchman professing to believe in the existence of a Church, when the most palpable facts must show him that no such Church exists; the "Low" Churchman professing to believe in exceptional interpositions which his philosophy secretly questions; the "Broad" Churchman professing as absolute an attachment to the Established Church as the narrowest could feel, while he is preaching such principles as will at last pull it down.

I ask you, my friend, whether there would not be more faith as well as earnestness, if all would speak out. There would be more unanimity too, because they would all agree in a certain basis. Would not a wider love supersede the creed-bound charity of sects?

I am aware that I have touched on a point of difference between us, and I will not regret it; for I think the differences of mind are analogous to those differences of nature, which, in the most comprehensive survey, are the very elements of harmony.

I am not at all prone to put forth my own opinions, but the tone in which you have written to me claims an unusual degree of openness on my part. I look upon creeds of all kinds as chains—far worse chains than those you would break—as the causes of much hypocrisy and infidelity. I hold it to be a sin to make a child say "I believe." Lead it to utter that belief spontaneously. I also consider the institution of an exclusive priesthood, though having been of service in some respects, as retarding the progress of Christianity at present. I desire to see a lay ministry.

I will not give you more of my heterodoxy at present; perhaps I need your pardon, connected as you are with the Church, for having said so much.

The headline of this newspaper clipping, one of several similar articles compiled in a nineteenth-century scrapbook, reads: *"Lady Byron Vindicated." Mrs. Stowe's Defence of Her Story and Herself. All Her "Facts" and "Proofs" Now Given. Why the Story was not Sooner Made Public. A Fresh Account of the Interview. Old Scandals, Letters, Reports and Rumors Revived and Reiterated.*

In August 1869, "The True Story of Lady Byron's Life" was published in the *Atlantic Monthly*. The story destroyed the notion that Lord Byron was a romantic, sensitive poet, and that Lady Byron was a cold, heartless woman who had rejected him. Information about Lord Byron's bad and often scandalous behavior was published for all to read. The public was not happy with what Harriet wrote about one of their beloved poets.

The reaction to the revealing article was very negative. Harriet was accused of creating a sensational story. Many were not interested in whether the accusations were right or wrong. They simply did not think the material should have been printed. Parliament debated briefly on whether to prevent Harriet from traveling to England. The *Atlantic Monthly* lost many subscribers just by printing the article.

Harriet was not discouraged by this reaction. She set about expanding her article and documenting her research into a book, and in 1870, *Lady Byron Vindicated* was published. Harriet drew more criticism with this book, and her reputation suffered even though many people knew that the stories about Lord Byron were true. The critics were also shocked that a lady would even discuss such things.

Although most men were critical of Harriet, the prominent women's rights activists Elizabeth Cady Stanton and Susan B. Anthony supported her. Stanton and Anthony admired Harriet Beecher Stowe and her

Elizabeth Cady Stanton is seated and Susan B. Anthony is standing in this portrait done around 1886. Their activism helped to bring about the Nineteenth Amendment to the Constitution, which finally gave women the right to vote in 1920.

talent, and wanted Harriet to write for the women's rights newspaper *Revolution*. Although Stowe supported women's rights, she declined to contribute to the newspaper *Revolution* or to speak publicly on women's rights issues. The reason for Harriet Beecher Stowe's refusal was due to her conservative view of women's rights that was anchored in her religious upbringing.

The women's rights movement led by Stanton and Anthony had its origins in the abolitionist movement. Men often denied women access to abolitionist groups and meetings. Women responded by organizing their own groups to fight both slavery and the restrictions that held women back. In some cases, women began to see slavery as a similar institution to marriage because both were created by men to restrict the freedom of others. Calling for an end to marriage was a position with which Harriet Beecher Stowe did not agree.

Nor did Harriet agree with the more radical ideas of the women's movement, promoted by such activists as Victoria Woodhull. In 1871, Harriet wrote another novel that was serialized in the *Christian Union*. This book highlighted the risks that the women's movement would take if it strayed too far from accepted conventions. The main character was based on Victoria Woodhull and was named Audacia Dangyereyes. In 1871, Harriet published another novel, *Pink and White Tyranny*, in which a husband is taken advantage of by his demanding wife, who wants everything her own way.

In 1872, Victoria Woodhull launched her own attack on the Beecher family. She accused Henry Ward Beecher of breaking his marriage vows. Henry Ward Beecher was Harriet's favorite brother and the most famous preacher in

Although Henry Ward Beecher tried to keep a low profile during the scandal, the press covered the affair for several years.

America at the time. His church in Brooklyn was always full of people who wanted to listen to his sermons, and he received high fees for his lectures. Woodhull's accusation that Henry might not be practicing the good behavior he recommended in his sermons came as a shock to the public.

Harriet came to the defense of her beloved brother, but the affair was mixed up in the women's rights

Isabella Beecher Hooker, Harriet's younger sister, photographed around 1841, threatened to voice her disapproval of her brother Henry at the Plymouth Church. To prevent this, Harriet sat in the front pew during services to intimidate Isabella should she try to carry out her threat.

issues of the day. It highlighted the double standard in which men had more rights and did not suffer as much in cases of immoral behavior as did women. Harriet's younger sister Isabella Beecher Hooker believed that the charges against Henry were true. Their disagreements over the charges against Henry Ward Beecher's character, caused a long rift between Harriet and Isabella. In the end, Henry Ward Beecher was cleared of all charges.

10. Her Final Years

As Harriet entered the sixtieth year of her life, she continued to write. In 1873, she published a series of stories called the *Palmetto Leaves*, based on her experiences in Florida. She also worked with Calvin to write *Women in Sacred History*, which was published in 1874. This book explored the lives of various women from the Bible. Her last novel was *Poganuc People*, which was published in 1878. In this novel, Harriet wrote a fictional story closely based on her memories as a child and schoolgirl in New England.

Harriet became a grandmother in 1870, when her daughter Georgiana May gave birth to a boy named Freeman. In 1873, the Stowe family moved into a more modest house in Hartford, Connecticut. Their neighbor, who moved to Hartford in 1874, was Samuel Langhorne Clemens. Many knew Samuel Clemens from his writing under the name Mark Twain.

Harriet was also invited to tour the country and give lectures and readings from her books in 1872. Traveling around the country was difficult for an older woman such

Harriet Beecher Stowe with her grandchildren Lyman and Leslie around 1885. Harriet held Lyman shortly after he was born and wrote, "He looked out of his blanket with large bright eyes & with apparent curiosity to know where he had got to & who I was." These were the children of Harriet's son Charles and his wife, Susan.

Samuel Clemens, who wrote under the pen name of Mark Twain, wrote *Huckleberry Finn* and *The Adventures of Tom Sawyer* while living in Hartford, Connecticut. This photo was taken around 1907.

as Harriet, but she said, "I get accustomed to it & the fatigue of railroad travel seems to do me good. I never sleep better than after a long days ride." Writing was Harriet's preferred method of communication, and she was not as strong a public speaker as her brother Henry. She did eventually become more confident in her speaking abilities, and she toured the country again in 1873.

Toward the end of the 1870s, Harriet gradually withdrew from public life. She spent time with Calvin, wrote letters to friends and family, and occasionally painted. In 1882, the *Atlantic Monthly* held a large celebration for Harriet's seventieth birthday. The day was actually her seventy-first birthday, but Harriet never publicly corrected the staff of the magazine. Many famous authors of the day who also contributed to the magazine were there to greet and congratulate Harriet.

Calvin and Harriet Stowe continued to travel to Mandarin, Florida, until 1884, when Calvin Stowe became sick. Harriet wrote that Calvin "has been more than ever an invalid, he is no longer able to walk out, and can do only a little reading & no writing." Harriet took care of Calvin until he died on August 6, 1886. When Calvin was in his old age, Harriet teased him and called him her "rabbi." Although the couple had sometimes had their difficulties, Harriet and Calvin had been happily married for fifty years.

While Harriet was taking care of Calvin, her twin daughters, Harriet, known as Hatty, and Eliza, took care of her. The twins had not married and spent their adult years helping their mother with her writing, travels, and housework. Harriet turned to her family after the loss of Calvin. Her strong family ties also helped her first in 1887, when the family suffered the loss of Henry Ward Beecher, her beloved brother, and then next in 1890, after the loss of Georgiana May, Harriet's daughter.

In 1889, Harriet suffered a serious stroke. She would recover physically, but not mentally. In 1893, she wrote to the author Oliver Wendell Holmes, "I am passing the last days of my life in the city where I passed my school-girl life. My physical health, since I recovered from my alarming illness, I had four years ago has been excellent. . . . My mental condition might be called nomadic." Surrounded by her family, Harriet Beecher Stowe died on July 1, 1896.

Harriet died shortly after her eighty-fifth birthday, after having lived through most of the upheaval and changes of the 1800s. She had risen to become one of the most highly paid, respected writers of her time. This was a major achievement, considering the barriers to women that she had overcome. Her output as an

Harriet Beecher Stowe at her desk in her home in Hartford in 1886.
After she retired, Harriet continued to attend reading circles, where
neighbors would gather to read books aloud, such as Charles
Dickens's *Bleak House*. The painting on the wall behind and to the
right of Harriet is a copy of Raphael's *Madonna of the Gold Finch*.

author was staggering. Harriet Beecher Stowe had more than thirty books and numerous articles published in her lifetime.

Harriet Beecher Stowe's most memorable and lasting work was *Uncle Tom's Cabin*. Critics in the twentieth century were less kind to this book, which remains her most famous novel. They point out weaknesses in the plot and characterizations, as well as her overly sentimental writing style. By today's standards the book has often been called racist in nature. She used broad characterizations to describe the black people in her novel, and often portrayed blacks as childlike. Harriet agreed with the paternalistic attitude taken toward blacks, and although she recognized them as human, she did not acknowledge them as equals.

Despite these criticisms, *Uncle Tom's Cabin* was the most important book of its time and had an enormous impact on people's views of slavery. Harriet clearly felt that the book needed to be written. In 1853 she wrote, "I must speak for the oppressed—who cannot speak for themselves."

Timeline

1811	Harriet Elizabeth Beecher is born on June 14 in Litchfield, Connecticut.
1816	Roxana Foote Beecher, Harriet's mother, dies after contracting tuberculosis.
1817	Lyman Beecher, Harriet's father, marries Harriet Porter.
1819–1824	Harriet attends Miss Pierce's School in Litchfield, Connecticut.
1824–1826	Harriet attends the Hartford Female Seminary, a school founded by her older sister, Catharine Beecher.
	In 1826, Lyman Beecher moves to Boston to take a job as pastor of the Hanover Street Church.
1827	Harriet returns from a brief stay in Boston and begins to teach at the Hartford Female Seminary.
1832	The Beecher family moves to Cincinnati, where Lyman Beecher becomes president of the Lane Theological Seminary and where Catharine Beecher establishes the Western Female Institute.
1833	Harriet visits a student in Kentucky, where she observes slavery firsthand. Harriet and Catharine write the textbook *Primary Geography for Children*. Harriet becomes friends with Eliza and Calvin Stowe.
1836	Harriet marries Calvin Stowe. Harriet observes three days of rioting in Cincinnati against an abolitionist newspaper.
1839	Harriet adds to the family income by publishing stories in national magazines.

	Calvin and Henry Ward Beecher help a former slave, who is working for them, escape via the Underground Railroad.
1845	Harriet Beecher Stowe writes the article "Immediate Emancipation" for an abolitionist newspaper.
1846	Harriet Beecher Stowe spends a year at a spa in Vermont to help restore her health.
1850	Calvin Stowe becomes a professor at Bowdoin College, and the family moves to Brunswick, Maine. Harriet Beecher Stowe vows to write about the evils of slavery after the passage of the Fugitive Slave Law.
1851	Stow writes installments, or chapters of *Uncle Tom's Cabin; or, Life Among the Lowly*. They are published in the *National Era*, a Washington, D.C., abolitionist paper.
1852	Calvin Stowe becomes a professor at the Andover Theological Seminary, and the family moves to Andover, Massachusetts. *Uncle Tom's Cabin* is published as a book by J. P. Jewett in Boston and sells three hundred thousand copies in the first year, earning Harriet Beecher Stowe approximately $10,000.
1853	*A Key to Uncle Tom's Cabin* is published. Harriet Beecher Stowe travels to Europe, where she is treated as a celebrity.
1856	*Dred: A Tale of the Great Dismal Swamp* is published.
1859	*The Minister's Wooing* is published.
1860	Abraham Lincoln is elected president. Seven states in the South form the Confederate States of America when they secede from the United States.
1861	The Civil War begins.
1862	*The Pearl of Orr's Island* and *Agnes of Sorrento* are published. Harriet Beecher Stowe meets President Abraham Lincoln.
1863	The Stowe family moves to Hartford, Connecticut, and Calvin Stowe retires from teaching. Lyman Beecher dies.

	President Lincoln signs the Emancipation Proclamation.
1865	The Civil War ends. President Lincoln is assassinated.
1868	The Stowes purchase a home in Mandarin, Florida, where they vacation in the winter.
1869	*Oldtown Folks* is published.
1870	*Lady Byron Vindicated* is published.
1872	Victoria Woodhull accuses Henry Ward Beecher of breaking his marriage vows.
1878	*Poganuc People*, Harriet Beecher Stowe's last novel, is published.
1882	Harriet Beecher Stowe celebrates her seventy-first birthday in Boston. The *Atlantic Monthly* throws a party in her honor.
1886	Calvin Stowe dies.
1896	Harriet Beecher Stowe dies of a stroke on July 1.

Glossary

abolition (a-buh-LIH-shun) The official ending of the practice of slavery.

boarder (BOR-der) One who pays rent to stay in a room, usually within a private home.

bolster (BOL-ster) To support.

cholera (KAH-luh-rah) A highly contagious and often fatal intestinal disease.

colloquial (kuh-LOH-kwee-ul) Conversational; using a conversational style that mimics everyday speech, particularly in writing.

composition (kom-puh-ZIH-shun) A piece of writing, especially a school exercise in the form of a brief essay.

condemnation (kon-dem-NAY-shun) Blame.

dialect (DY-uh-lekt) A kind of language spoken only in a certain area.

emancipation (ih-man-sih-PAY-shun) The act of freeing from the restraint, control, or power of another; usually referring to the freeing of slaves.

eulogy (YOO-luh-jee) A speech of praise, usually given at a funeral.

evangelist (ih-VAN-juh-list) A person who preaches about Jesus and the Gospels.

fatigue (fuh-TEEG) Extreme tiredness or lack of energy; exhaustion.

immorality (ih-mor-AH-lih-tee) Being against generally held principles of behavior or morals.

lassitude (LA-suh-tood) The condition of weariness or lethargy.

natural philosophy (NA-chuh-rul fih-LAH-suh-fee) Any of the sciences that deal with matter or energy, such as physics, chemistry, or biology.

ordained (or-DAYND) To have given someone a position in a church as a preacher.

paternalistic (puh-ter-nul-IS-tik) Referring to a system in which authorities care for and regulate those in their control.

philanthropist (fih-LAN-thruh-pist) One who practices goodwill toward others; a charitable person.

plantation (plan-TAY-shun) A very large farm. During the 1700s and the 1800s, many plantation owners used slaves to work on these farms.

revival (rih-VY-vul) A period of new religious interest, or a series of evangelical meetings.

royalties (ROY-ul-teez) Payments made to an author for each copy of his or her work sold.

salvation (sal-VAY-shun) To be saved. In religion, to be saved from evil, or to be admitted to heaven through faith in God or through one's good works.

scandalous (SKAN-duhl-us) Referring to conduct or behavior thought to be improper or immoral.

seminary (SEH-mih-ner-ee) An institution of secondary or higher education.

serialized (SEER-ee-uh-lyzd) To have been arranged or published in successive parts or installments rather than all at once.

stamina (STA-mih-nuh) The ability to work hard for a long time.

supplement (SUH-pluh-ment) To add to something.

temperance (TEM-puh-rents) Moderation in or abstinence from the use of intoxicating drinks such as alcohol.

Additional Resources

If you would like to learn more about Harriet Beecher Stowe, check out the following books and Web sites:

Books

Coil, Suzanne M. *Harriet Beecher Stowe*. New York: Franklin Watts, 1993.

Fritz, Jean. *Harriet Beecher Stowe and the Beecher Preachers*, New York: G. P. Putnam's Sons, a division of The Putnam & Grosset Group, 1994.

Jakoubek, Robert E. *Harriet Beecher Stowe*. Philadelphia: Chelsea House Publishers, 1989.

Web Sites

Due to the changing nature of Internet links, PowerPlus Books has developed an online list of Web sites related to the subject of this book. This site is updated regularly. Please use this link to access the list: www.powerkidslinks.com/lalt/hbstowe/

Bibliography

Ammons, Elizabeth, ed. *Critical Essays on Harriet Beecher Stowe.* Boston: G. K. Hall, 1980.

Crozier, Alice C. *The Novels of Harriet Beecher Stowe.* New York: Oxford University Press, 1969.

Foster, Charles H. *The Rungless Ladder: Harriet Beecher Stowe and New England Puritanism.* Durham, NC: Duke University Press, 1970.

Hedrick, Joan D. *Harriet Beecher Stowe, A Life.* New York: Oxford University Press, 1994.

Kirkham, E. Bruce. *The Building of "Uncle Tom's Cabin."* Knoxville, TN: University of Tennessee Press, 1977.

Rugoff, Milton. *The Beechers: An American Family in the Nineteenth Century.* New York: Harper & Row, 1981.

Stowe, Charles Edward, ed. *The Life of Harriet Beecher Stowe Compiled from Her Letters and Journals.* Boston: Houghton Mifflin, 1889.

Stowe, Harriet Beecher. *Harriet Beecher Stowe: Three Novels.* Katherine Kish Sklar, ed. New York: Literary Classics of the United States, 1982. (Originally published in 1869.)

Index

About the Author

Ryan P. Randolph is a freelance writer with an avid interest in history. Ryan has a Bachelor of Arts degree in both history and political science from Colgate University in Hamilton, New York. He has written several history books for children. He currently works in a strategic consulting and research firm that specializes in the financial services industry. He lives with his wife in Mount Vernon, New York.

About the Consultant

Dawn C. Adiletta is the curator of the Harriet Beecher Stowe Center in Hartford, Connecticut. Dawn has a Master of Arts in U.S. history and has worked in the museum field for more than twenty years. The Harriet Beecher Stowe Center is the site of Stowe's 1871 Victorian cottage, a prestigious research library, and gift shop. The Center preserves Harriet Beecher Stowe's Hartford home and its historic contents, provides a forum for the vibrant discussion of her life and work, and inspires individuals to embrace Stowe's commitment to social justice and to work toward positive change in their communities.

Primary Sources

Cover: *Harriet Beecher Stowe*. Alanson Fisher, Oil on canvas, 1853, National Portrait Gallery, Smithsonian Institution. Background, first edition title page of *Uncle Tom's Cabin*, Harriet Beecher Stowe, published in 1852 by John P. Jewett & Company, Boston, Rare Book and Special Collections Division, Library of Congress. **Page 4**: *Harriet Beecher Stowe*. Engraved by the National Bank Note Company, New York, 1864–1866, Harriet Beecher Stowe Center. **Page 7**: *$200 Reward Ran away from the subscriber . . . Five Negro Slaves*, Broadside, 1847, Library of Congress, Rare Book and Special Collections Division. **Page 13**: Wood panel with tulip decoration. Oil on wood, from the Litchfield Congregational Church pulpit, Litchfield Historical Society. **Page 18**: *View of the Litchfield Female Academy*. Attributed to Napoleon Gimbrede, watercolor and ink, 1830, Litchfield Historical Society. **Page 19**: *Catharine Beecher*, photo, ca.1860, Schlesinger Library, Radcliffe Institute, Harvard University. **Page 20**: *Hartford Female Seminary, Hartford, CT*, engraving, ca. 1862, Harriet Beecher Stowe Center. **Page 22**: *Primary Geography for Children*, by Catharine Beecher and Harriet Beecher. Engraving by E. Latella, 1833, Harriet Beecher Stowe Center. **Page 24**: *Georgiana May Allen*, photo, ca. 1865, Harriet Beecher Stowe Center. **Page 26**: *Democratic ticket. Going the whole hog. An illustrated election ticket for Martin Van Buren and Richard M. Johnson, listing Ohio Democratic electors for the presidential race of 1836*, Wood: engraving and letterpress, 1836, Library of Congress Rare Book and Special Collections Division. **Page 27**: *The Drunkard's Progress, or The Direct Road to Poverty, Wretchedness & Ruin*; shown is *The Confirmed Drunkard*. Hand-colored engraving, designed and published by J. W. Barber, 1826, Library of Congress Prints and Photographs Division. **Page 28**: *Cincinnati in 1837, Die vierte Strasse, von Vine Strasse westlich,. "Fourth St. looking west from Vine."* Hand-colored print, 1837, Ohio Historical Society. **Page 31**: *Eliza Tyler Stowe*. Oil on canvas, Hoyt, posthumous portrait, ca. 1852, Harriet Beecher Stowe Center. Page 34: *Map of Prussia*. From *W. M. Higgins's General Descriptive Atlas of the Earth*, Hand-colored copperplate engraving, John Dower, published by Orr and Smith, 1836. **Page 35**: *Eliza and Harriet Stowe*. Photo, ca. 1860s, Harriet Beecher Stowe Center. **Page 38**: Fashion plate from *Godey's Ladies' Book*, hand-colored engraving, 1839, Harriet Beecher Stowe Center. **Page 39**: Harriet Beecher Stowe and Calvin Stowe, Daguerreotype, G. K. Warren, 1852, Schlesinger Library, Radcliffe Institute, Harvard University. **Page 41**: Harriet Beecher Stowe's Medicine Kit. Harriet Beecher Stowe Center. **Page 42**: *The Water Cure Journal and Herald of Reforms for 1854*, Back cover, 1854, Library of Congress Rare Book and Special Collections Division. **Page 43**: *Samuel Charles Stowe*. Daguerreotype, July 1848, Fontayne & Porter's Gallery, Schlesinger Library, Radcliffe Institute, Harvard University. **Page 46**: Slave houses on Hermitage plantation, Savannah, Georgia. Photographic print, Walker Evans, February 1935, Farm Security Administration Collection, Library of Congress Prints and Photographs Division. **Page 47**: Illustrations of the *Anti-Slavery Almanac for 1840*, New York: American Anti-Slavery Society, 1840. Broadside, engraving and type, 1840, Rare Book and Special Collections Division, Library of Congress. **Page 51**: *Effects of the Fugitive-Slave Law*. Lithograph,

Theodore Kaufmann, 1850, New York: Hoff & Bloede, Library of Congress Prints and Photographs Division. **Page 55**: *Uncle Tom's Cabin* by Harriet Beecher Stowe. Title page, 1852, London: John Cassell, Rare Book and Special Collections Division, Library of Congress. **Page 57**: *Webb's Characters & Scenes in Uncle Tom's Cabin*, Plate 9. Hand-colored woodcut, 1850, Harriet Beecher Stowe Center. **Page 64**: *Frederick Douglass*. Oil on canvas, 1844, National Portrait Gallery, S.I./Art Resource. **Page 65**: *Charles Edward Stowe*. Photo, ca. 1875–1880, Harriet Beecher Stowe Center. **Page 66**: *"Uncle Tom & Eva"* Poster, lithograph, color, ca. 1899, Courier Litho. Co, Theatrical Poster Collection, Library of Congress Prints and Photographs. **Page 67**: *A Key to Uncle Tom's Cabin*, Harriet Beecher Stowe. Title page, 1853, Boston, J. P. Jewett, General Research Division, New York Public Library, Astor, Lenox, and Tilden Foundations. **Page 70**: Map of Europe from the *Royal Illustrated Atlas*. Colored lithograph, 1862, published in London by A. H. Fullarton. **Page 71**: *Beecher Family*, photo, Mathew Brady, ca. 1859, Harriet Beecher Stowe Center. **Page 72**: *John Brown of Osawatomie*, Painted mural in the Kansas State capitol, John Steuart Curry, 1937–1941, Kansas State Historical Society. **Page 73**: *Beecher Bible*. Engraving of Sharps carbine rifle from an advertisement, ca. 1850s, Kansas State Historical Society. **Page 74**: *Dred, a Tale By the Author of Uncle Tom's Cabin*, cover, 1856, British edition, Harriet Beecher Stowe Center. **Page 75**: *Henry Ellis Stowe*, Photo, ca. 1852, Harriet Beecher Stowe Center. **Page 77**: *Frederick Stowe*. Photo, ca. 1861, Harriet Beecher Stowe Center. **Page 78**: *Abraham Lincoln with Harriet Beecher Stowe*. Charcoal on paper, Harry Everett Townsend, New Britain Museum of American Art, Gift of James H. Dougherty. **Page 79**: *The battle of Gettysburg, Pa. July 3d. 1863*. Lithograph, hand-colored, ca. 1863, New York : Published by Currier & Ives, Library of Congress Prints and Photographs Division. **Page 82**: *The Pearl of Orr's Island* by Harriet Beecher Stowe. Title page, 1862, Library of Congress Rare Book and Special Collections Division. **Page 85**: *Stowe Family Home, Mandarin, Florida*. Photo mounted on wood, oil paint and textile fringe, ca. 1874, Harriet Beecher Stowe Center. **Page 87**: *Lady Byron*. Engraving, ca. 1830s, Hulton/Getty/Achive. **Page 88**: *"Lady Byron Vindicated."* Newsprint clippings, Harriet Beecher Stowe Center. **Page 90**: Elizabeth Cady Stanton and Susan B. Anthony, photo, ca. 1886, Library of Congress Prints and Photographs Division **Page 91**: *Henry Ward Beecher*, photo, James Wadsworth Family Papers, Library of Congress Manuscript Division. **Page 92**: *Isabella Beecher Hooker*. Daguerreotype, ca. 1841, Harriet Beecher Stowe Center. **Page 95**: *Harriet Beecher Stowe with her grandchildren*. Photo, ca. 1885, Harriet Beecher Stowe Center. **Page 96**: *Samuel Langhorne Clemens*, Photographic print, 1907, Library of Congress Prints and Photographs Division. **Page 98-99**: *Harriet Beecher Stowe at Home* in Hartford. Photo, 1886, Harriet Beecher Stowe Center.

Credits

Photo Credits

Cover (portrait), pp. 4, 10, 11, 20, 22, 24, 30, 31, 35, 38, 58–59, 65, 71, 74, 75, 77, 85, 88, 92, 95, 98–99 courtesy of the Harriet Beecher Stowe Center, Hartford, CT; cover (background image) pp. 7, 26, 42, 47, 55, 82 Library of Congress Rare Book and Special Collections Division; pp. 13, 18 Collection of the Litchfield Historical Society, Litchfield, Connecticut; p. 14 © Thomas P. Benincas, Jr.; pp. 19, 39, 43 the Schlesinger Library, Radcliffe Institute, Harvard University; pp. 27, 46, 51, 66, 79, 90, 96 Library of Congress Prints and Photographs Division; pp. 28, 49 Ohio Historical Society; p. 41 courtesy of the Harriet Beecher Stowe Center, Hartford, CT, photo by Maura B. McConnell; p. 56 © Historical Picture Archive/CORBIS; p. 61 photograph courtesy Peabody Essex Museum; p. 64 National Portrait Gallery, Smithsonian Institution/Art Resource, New York; p. 67 General Research Division, New York Public Library, Astor, Lenox, and Tilden Foundations; pp. 72, 73 Kansas State Historical Society; p. 78 New Britain Museum of American Art, Connecticut, Gift of James H. Dougherty; p. 87 © Hulton/Archive; p. 91 Library of Congress Manuscript Division, James Wadsworth Family Papers.

Project Editor
Daryl Heller

Series Design
Laura Murawski

Layout Design
Corinne L. Jacob

Photo Researcher
Jeffrey Wendt